THE QUIRKS OF CHORLTON-CUM-HARDY

A HISTORY OF ITS PEOPLE AND PLACES
Andrew Simpson & Peter Topping

TOPPER PUBLISHING

About the Authors

First published 2017.

Topper Publishing
39 Lambton Road, Chorlton-cum-Hardy,
Manchester, M21 0ZJ.
Tel: 0161 718 0193

Copyright © 2017 Andrew Simpson & Peter Topping.

The right of Andrew Simpson & Peter Topping to be identified as the Authors of this work has been asserted in accordance with the Copyrights, Designs and Patents Act 1988.

ISBN 978 0 995705 54 8

Peter Topping and Andrew Simpson have been working together for a number of years developing projects linked to the history of South Manchester. It is, as Peter said, a collaboration where he paints the pictures and Andrew tells the stories. Their work has appeared in venues across South Manchester, including an 80 metre mural, which was commissioned by a large building company and opened by Lord Bradley of Withington in 2012. Peter and Andrew also work independently.

Peter's work is much admired and he regularly exhibits his work, showcasing it on his website at www.paintingsfrompictures.co.uk

Andrew writes extensively on a range of historical subjects, contributing to various publications including Canadian ones and produces a popular history blog at www.chorltonhistory.blogspot.co.uk His books include a study of rural Chorlton in the 19th century, a book on Manchester in the Great War and he has been commissioned to write the history of a well known children's charity.

Together Peter and Andrew have written Didsbury Through Time, Hough End Hall The Story, Manchester Pubs - City Centre and Manchester Pubs - Chorlton-cum-Hardy.

All rights reserved. No part of this book may be reprinted or reproduced or utilised in any form or by any electronic, mechanical or other means, now known or hereafter invented, including photocopying and recording, or in any information storage or retrieval system, without the permission in writing from the Publishers.

British Library Cataloguing in Publication Data.
A catalogue record for this book is available from the British Library.

Typesetting and origination by Topper Publishing
Printed in Great Britain.

Contents

About the Authors — 2

Acknowledgements — 4

Introduction — 5

THE OLD CHORLTON — 8
Some farms, some pubs, a church and school, and a collection of cottages.

Chorlton Green... Chorlton Evangelical Church... The Lych Gate and village graveyard... Angus Bateman and an archaeological dig... Chorlton Row, the lane out of the village... Mr Sharp's superior house... Etchells and Beech Road Takeaway... Marjorie Holmes 1921-2014... The Living Legend that is Dave the Butcher... Sutton's Cottage... Beech House...

CHORLTONVILLE — 54
And the estate to the east.

Quentin Crisp... Steve Pullen MBE... Chorltonville... The Stumps and other things... East from the "Ville and on till morning or Darley Avenue, whichever comes first... George Best..

SOUTHERN CEMETERY — 78
A magical place of wildlife, fascinating history and powerful memories.

A new cemetery for the south of the city, fit for purpose... Sir John Alcock... Sir Matt Busby... Sir John Rylands... Wilfred Pickles... L. S. Lowry...

BARLOW MOOR ROAD — 94
And on to Manchester Road.

Chorlton Park, and more than a few surprises... Leon's, the date and a mystery... The cinemas, just 80 and a bit years of flickering magic... Essoldo... Palais de Luxe... Gaumont... The Pavilion... Foster's, cycles, a dairy and a muriel... Kemp's Corner... The Library, "built in fulfilment of a promise made in 1904"... Unicorn, a Chorlton co-operative since 1996 with a roof garden and pond... Chorlton Swimming Baths, a second promise fulfilled...

EDGE LANE AND WILBRAHAM ROAD — 134
The ancient and the modern.

That place over the railway track, beyond the Dukes Canal, Stretford... Longford House, and our own Chorlton radical... Westonby and The Twilight Sleep Home for painless child birth... Reaching out to the community... Highfield, numbers 2 to 18 Wilbraham Road, the shops with a secret... The Post office, that letter box and a story about The Blitz... Over the railway bridge, past Egerton Arcade and then to the Creameries...

ALL OF FAME — 164
Being a collection of those who lived, still live or passed through Chorlton.

Alan Hollingum... Joe Mercer, the letter helping him with his team selection and other notable football chaps... Alan Brown and a century of the Chorlton Brass Band... Steve Raw... Kingbee records and a wealth of musical talent... The Bee Gees... Badly Drawn Boy... Midge Addy, a remarkable woman... Stan, Mona, Chris and Lyn, at the Trevor... Lipservice...

Epilogue — 194

Acknowledgements

We would like to thank everyone that was involved in the research that went into the making of this book, especially Manchester Libraries, Information and Archives, Manchester City Council who gave us permission to use the black & white images throughout the book and the Digital Archives Association for supplying the old Chorlton maps.

We would also like to thank the following people in no particular order whose knowledge and research into this book was extremely valuable. Allan Brown, Alan Hollingum, Andy Robertson, Angus Bateman, Ann Love, Chorlton Good Neighbours, Chorlton Journal, Chris & Lyn, Claude-Étienne Armingaud, Collette Books, Daily Worker, David O'Reilly, Digital Archives Association, www.digitalarchives.co.uk, Doug Currie, David Wilkinson, East Dunbartonshire Archive, Egerton Papers, England Coach Post Card, Graham Gill, Jillian Goldsmith, JT, Ken Foster, Majorie Holmes, Manchester Libraries, Information and Archives, Manchester City Council, Old Football Pictures, Philip Lloyd, Rev John Booker, Rita Bishop, Robert Walker, Sapfo, Stephen Raw, Steve Pullen, The Building News, The Lloyd Collection, Tony Goulding, Tony Walker, Tuck DB Postcards, www.tuckdb.org, Turf Cigarette cards, Lipservice, Paul Maylor, David Harrop, Ann Love, Ida Bradshaw, Chris Hall and Bob Jones.

And especially Lindy Newns, who again spent many hours proofreading and editing the copy.

Andrew would like to thank Tina and his four sons who patiently listened to each exciting new story asked the right questions and always showed interest and offered encouragement.

And Peter would like to thank his Wife Linda for her understanding, and help with yet another book.

Also we would like to apologise for anyone we have missed in this Acknowledgement.

Introduction

What was once a quiet country village is being rapidly transformed into a town... and it is desirable to place on record its early characteristics, and gather up such traditions as should reveal the condition of bygone times before the links connecting those old days with the present should be broken".[1]

These were pretty much the final words our own local historian wrote in concluding his History of Chorlton-cum-Hardy. It had taken him 26 articles spread out over the winter and spring of 1885-6 and drew on a variety of historical records, traditions and a pool of memories which went back beyond the loss of the American colonies to a time when we were a small rural community.

Those traditions included the "harvest home", the rush spreading ceremonies, and characters like Caleb Jodrell, who was a ringleader in the ancient custom of Riding the Stang, and Mary Crowther who was the last woman to do penance in front of the altar of the parish church.[2]

All have been documented in the more recent history of Chorlton in the early 19th century, which described those rural traditions and a way of life, which by the 1860s was already disappearing.[3]

And now it is time to look at some of the more recent traditions, and personalities of the last half century and a bit of Chorlton's history.

It began with a discussion on what made Chorlton different, and quickly moved away from the plethora of bars and interesting places to eat, briefly fastening on our own theatre company, and eventually settled on things you didn't know about Chorlton, and probably didn't know whom to ask.

Living in a town with a quirky name like Chorlton-cum-Hardy, what else could we call the book except... The Quirks of Chorlton-cum-Hardy, and while some things are indeed very

---

1 Ellwood, Thomas, Chapter XXVI, The Story of Chorlton-cum-Hardy, South Manchester Gazette, May 15, 1886
2 The custom of Riding the Stang or Rough Music, was a practice which dates back to the Middle Ages and was common across Europe and involved the public humiliation of wrong doers.
3 Simpson, Andrew, The Story of Chorlton-cum-Hardy, 2012

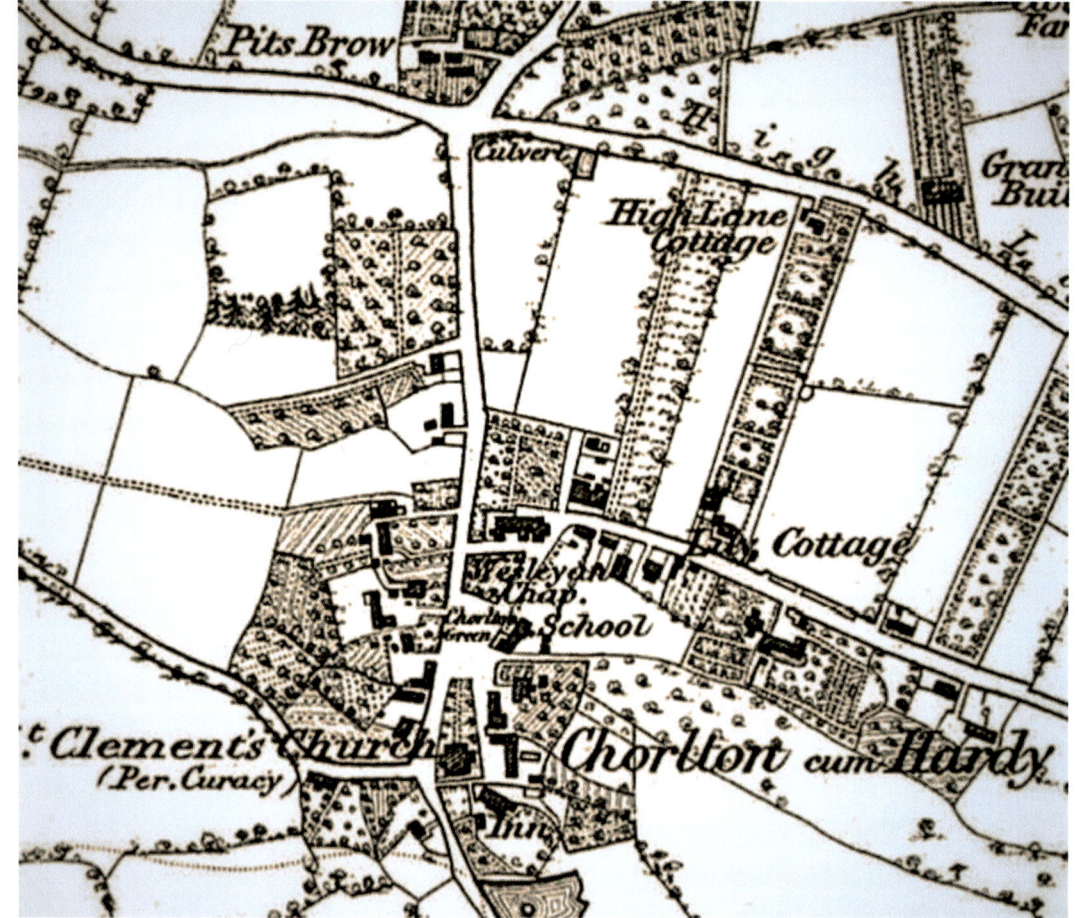

Chorlton and the Row 1854

odd, bordering on the bizarre, others are just a tad eccentric; into the pot we also dropped people who have made a contribution to the township, or who are, or were, much loved personalities.

We don't claim it is an exhaustive collection and, while there will be those who mutter about who or what we have left out, we are pleased with what's been included.

And like our two pubs books, we have designed Quirks, both as a story to be read in front of the fire, or as a series of walks, taking the intrepid seeker to all things quirky across Chorlton, from east to west and back again.[1]

At which point, it is perhaps incumbent on me to mention the geography of where we live, which was bounded by the River Mersey and the flood plain to the south and the neighbouring townships on the other three sides.

> Dear Andy,
> Well you did ask! So don't blame me if I have burdened you with more information than you really wanted. What started off as scraps of notes took me over and snowballed, and I must admit I've thoroughly enjoyed myself without having to move much further than my armchair.

Letter from Marjorie 2010

    Nor were we just Chorlton, because, as the old name of Chorlton-cum-Hardy suggests, some of us lived in Chorlton, others in Hardy and some more in Martledge. Chorlton was the largest hamlet and was situated around the village green on the edge of the flood plain. As for the others, Hardy was out by the Mersey, and Martledge was roughly a little north of the junction of Wilbraham and Barlow Moor Roads.

    The last cottages at Hardy were abandoned in the middle of the 19th century, and Martledge disappeared during the housing boom of the late 19th century.

    So complete was Martledge's disappearance under rows of new houses and shops that the name also disappeared, and it became known as New Chorlton, or the New Village, to distinguish it from old Chorlton, which remained more rural.

    But my friend Marjorie never took to New Chorlton, and remained convinced that it would better to retain that older name of Martledge.

    And that, it seems to me, is the first of our interesting and quirky bits of information, and holds out the promise that later we will revisit this lost place, and make the connection between Marjorie and those people she often dismissed as, "all fancy cakes and silk knickers".

1 Topping Peter, Simpson Andrew, Manchester Pubs, The Stories Behind the Doors, City Centre, 2016, and Chorlton, 2017

THE OLD CHORLTON
Some farms, some pubs, a church and school, and a collection of cottages.

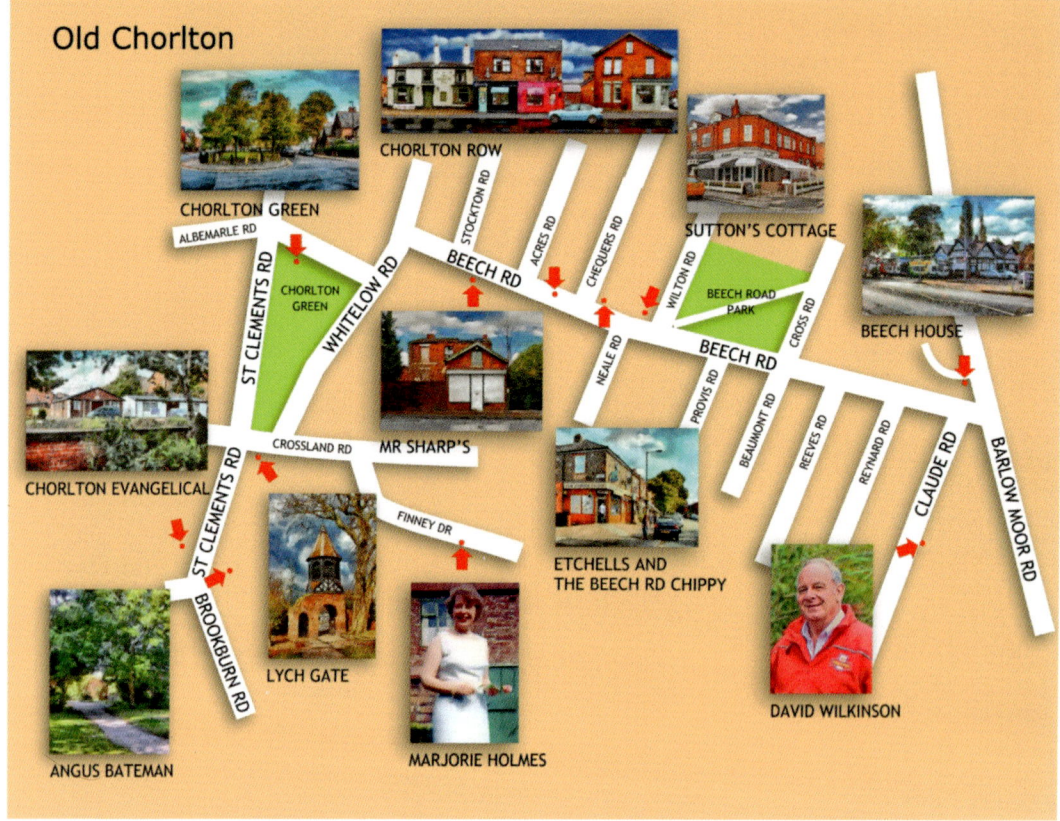

The area surrounding Chorlton Green and what is now Beech Road was the centre of old Chorlton and was larger than its neighbouring hamlets of Hardy and Martledge.

And superficially it maintains that image of a rural settlement with its village green, old parish church yard and school, along with two farmhouses and of course those two pubs.

But as we shall see, for nearly a century the village green was lost to its villagers, our picturesque lych gate was only built in 1887 and the half timbered appearance of the Horse and Jockey was only added in the 1920s.

Added to this, the village school closed long ago and, after a period as a factory followed by offices, it underwent a conversion into residential properties.

Nor does it stop there. The water fountain, once a feature of the village green, followed its ornate drinking cups and was scrapped, and even the telephone kiosk, much loved by all who either didn't have a phone or wanted a romantic assignation, was moved from the centre of the green to a corner and has now also been lost.

And those looking for the two village ponds will be equally disappointed. The one beside the Bowling Green vanished in the late 19th century and the second, which ran the length of Chorlton Row, was filled in to make way for a row of shops in the 1870s.

Even the name Chorlton Row, which was what the lane out of the village had always been called, was summarily changed to the pedestrian name of Beech Road.

But not all has been lost. During the late 1970s and early '80s, a series of archaeological digs uncovered something of the history of the parish church, and more recently there has been a reawakened interest in our rural past.

The books of John Lloyd, and Cliff Hayes have dug deep into the oral testimonies from the 18th and early 19th centuries, which were collected by Thomas Ellwood in the 1880s. More recently Andrew Simpson's book used these folk memories, along with a wealth of other original source material, to recreate the Chorlton of the first half of the 19th century.[1]

And there is also our own blog site devoted to the history of the township, which ranges over Chorlton's past and attracts a varied group of contributors, who share their photographs and memories of Chorlton's past.[2]

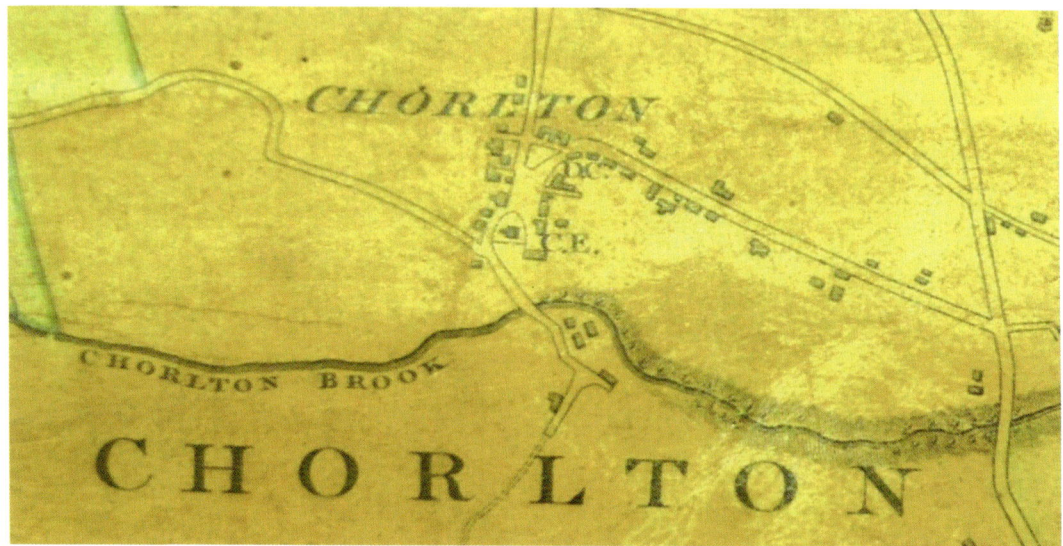

Chorlton circa late 18th century

1 Simpson, Andrew, The Story of Chorlton-cum-Hardy, 2012
2 Chorltonhistoryblogspot, https://chorltonhistory.blogspot.co.uk/

Chorlton Green 1928

Chorlton Green...

the heart of the village and once Mr Wilton's own private garden.

Now the old village green is not what it seems, not least because, for nearly a century, it was the private garden of the Wilton family, who lived in what is now part of the Horse and Jockey.

Just how Samuel Wilton acquired the Green in the early 19th century is unclear, but acquire it he did and, to make sure it remained private, he planted thick hedges around its boundary, which effectively closed it off to the residents of the village until the death of his daughter in 1895, whereupon the land reverted to the Egerton estate, which gifted it as a public space.

Chorlton Green circa 1900

And, for a long while afterwards, the restored green was, in fact, not green but stone, having been given a hard surface, but it did, as a compensation, have a water fountain, which once had a collection of drinking cups.

Shop and Horse & Jockey 1935

Long before Mr Wilton's land grab, the Green was the site of much that passed for rural entertainment, including bull baiting, the annual Wakes ceremonies and the custom of pace egging, where at Easter, a group of the younger villagers would dress up and act out the story of St George triumphing over his enemies. Dressed "with cardboard, tinsel, ribbon, calico, &c., of various colours, and presenting a very gaudy appearance, [they] would set off on the dawn of Good Friday for a tour of the village and the surrounding district, calling at the farmsteads, various residences, and public-houses, the occupants of which, expecting the call, were quite prepared to receive them. The company comprised "Open the Door", "Saint George", "Bold Slasher", "Black Morocco King", "Doctor", "Doubt", and "The Devil", and each carried a sword, with the exception of the doctor, who carried a large stick and bottle. One of the number known as Tosspot was dressed as a lady, whose duty it was to carry the basket for the receipt of eggs and other gifts".[1]

Chorlton Green 1925

[1] Ellwood, Thomas, Chapter 8, Pace Egging, December 12 1885, History of Chorlton-cum-Hardy, South Manchester Gazette, 1885-86

Chorlton Evangelical Church...
the small place of worship facing the old parish church.

Now I have always been fascinated by the small building which is Chorlton Evangelical Church and I am indebted to Mr Paul Maylor for its story.

He told me that before the present building was constructed, the worshippers used the large room above the old grocer's shop on the corner of Beech Road and Wilton Road, which in time became a launderette, and is now Launderette bar cafe.

"The picture of the church building dates from sometime soon after the opening in December 1951 and the change of name to Chorlton Evangelical Church.

This is the original building and the white hall which is at the side of the building today wasn't built until the 1960s".[1]

Evangelical Church 1976

The Launderette 2017

1 Mr Paul Maylor, 2017

The Lych Gate and village graveyard...

being a collection of tales, including a nasty little quarrel, the Great Burial Scandal and the lost skull.

Lych gate & St Clement's 1903

Today the Green offers up quite a few interesting buildings, from the two pubs that face each other, to the village school and Mr Higginbotham's farm house and barn, while for those with slightly longer memories there is Spark's garage and that red telephone kiosk.

But for some, the most memorable building is the lych gate which stands at the northern end of the old parish churchyard. It seems to play its part in what looks to be a very traditional rural scene, and yet it only dates back to 1887 and the old Queen's Jubilee, and is as much a testament to a bitter local quarrel as it is to Victoria's half century on the throne.

To understand that quarrel and the degree it split the community we have to step back another twenty years, when it

Spark's garage and Chorlton Green 1976

19

Lych gate & St Clement's circa 1900

became clear that the old parish church had grown too small to accommodate Chorlton's growing population.

Most seemed agreed on the need for a new building, but, as ever, the devil was in the detail. Some favoured a spot just to the west of the existing church, but everything was thrown into the air by an offer from the Egerton estate of a plot of land where High Lane and Edge Lane meet.

Those who favoured the Edge Lane site went ahead, raised money for a building fund and, in the fullness of time, oversaw the construction of a new church, at which point the congregation was split, with some of the more influential preferring the old parish church by the Green.

The upshot was that the old church remained the parish church, till its closure in 1940 and final demolition in 1949.

Those who favoured the old church lavished money on both the building and a new and very impressive window, which was installed in the apse, and the church yard got its picturesque gate.

And along the way it became involved in the Great Burial Scandal, which is a pretty gruesome tale, and difficult to comprehend as you walk through the old parish graveyard on a warm spring day.

But back in 1881 it was, according to some, so full that, "it is now difficult to tell where there is any land left for new graves, [and because] so many internments have taken place there is not 2ft of earth between the coffin and the surface".[1]

There were also lurid tales of existing gravestones being broken up and thrown into the midden of the Bowling Green Hotel to allow new ones to be erected, and worse still, of bones and skulls appearing and being transported away in wheelbarrows.

Much more was revealed at the official Government inquiry opened by the Home Office in the November of 1881. One witness spoke of "human bones... knocking about the highway. Only that morning a jawbone with teeth in had been picked up".

There were also past sextons who reported the difficulty in finding space to place a coffin and the ever present danger of unearthing past burials. William Caldwell described how he regularly "disturbed human remains in digging" and once

Lych gate & St Clement's 1921

1 From the Chorlton Ratepayer Association to the Withington Local Board of Health January 12th 1881.
References from the Manchester Guardian 1881-86, Manchester City Council Town Clerks' Papers Re Closed Burial Grounds 1930, reports in the dig by Angus Batemean.

St Clements circa 1890

before he "could get down to any depth I smashed into another grave, and I was flooded by liquor and human remains".

Now, given that the first parish church had been opened in 1512, it should perhaps not be surprising that the place teemed with the dead. As the Reverend Booth admitted, while the burial records only dated back to 1753, he had come across a headstone from 1660, and confirmed "that the burial ground had been enlarged three times". Moreover "the interior of the church was filled with graves and the worshippers, Sunday by Sunday, knelt in the dust of their fathers".

Medical opinion increasingly turned on the health issue, which was compounded by the rapid growth in the population of the township.

But the real scandal seemed to be that the local church authorities had continued to bury the dead in the church, with the present sexton denying that there was a problem, and the

Reverend Booth being critical of the evidence of previous sextons, despite plenty of evidence that, for a decade or more, finding new spaces was difficult.

Of course we should temper our shock and disgust a little and remember the practice of removing old burials to accommodate new was a traditional practice.

Also I do have some sympathy with the argument made out by Reverend Booth and some correspondents to the Manchester Guardian, that for those with family plots, there was a real link with wanting also to be buried in the parish church.

But the Home Office Inspector was "satisfied that the churchyard is exceedingly full and that you want an order for the closing of the churchyard and the only thing to talk about is the exceptions".

The following year this was carried out with the proviso that, where families had an existing grave, an internment could go ahead, providing that the graves could be opened to a depth of five feet, without exposing coffins or disturbing human remains.

Finally, in 1930, the remains were exhumed and reburied in Southern Cemetery, which I suppose should have ended the matter, were it not for the discovery of some body parts during the archaeological dig in the late 1970s and early 80s, but that is another story.

Painting from a photo by Andrew Simpson

Angus Bateman and an archaeological dig...

uncovering centuries of our history, including an unexpected body and falling back on Gray's Anatomy.

The parish church yard was the subject of several archaeological digs by Angus Bateman, who lived close to the church yard in a 1960s development, which replaced the farm, small smithy and workshops, bordering the Green to the east of the church.

While his main interest was the churchyard and its church, he did see the need to develop the surrounding area in a way that retained the original village character and, to this end from 1965, pushed for the City Council to incorporate the Green and church yard, in an integrated plan of improvement.

He began "*some exploratory and very amateurish digs, at weekends, intermittently between October 1970 and August 1972*",[1] and concluded that he needed to gain more experience in running a dig, and to this end enrolled in a course in archaeology at Manchester University. The subsequent 1977 dig formed the project for that certificate and led on to further digs, culminating in the 1980-81 season, which was carried out with South Trafford Archaeological Group.[2]

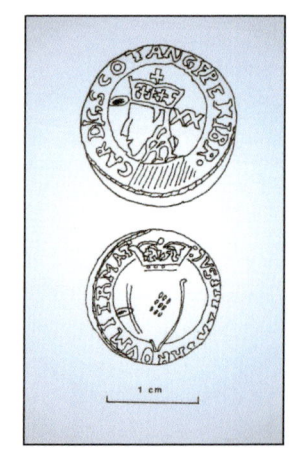
A find from the dig

The excavations and the subsequent research undertaken by Angus have helped with an understanding of the two churches which stood on the site from about 1512 till

1949, and a possible dating sequence for the extension of the graveyard in the early nineteenth century. The fragments from the later church were carefully analysed and recorded and, in some cases, Angus was able to track the manufacturers, some of whom were still trading in the 1970s. He also undertook a very detailed record of all the gravestones, including an analysis of the style and composition of the inscriptions, and some work on the light they threw on life expectancy amongst the young in the township.

And there are the everyday personal possessions which were revealed. Sadly, these are now missing, but they were carefully recorded, and they are the stuff of everyday life.

Most of the finds date from the 19th century. The

Searching for 16th century St Clement's

IN THE heart of old Chorlton under the shadow of a modern super development of two-bedroomed flats, amateur archaeologists are digging up part of Chorlton Green graveyard in search of evidence of the first St Clement's Church.

Led by Mr Angus Bateman of Finney Drive, the South Trafford Archaeological Group (STAG) have already turned over half the top soil on the site of the 16th century church. The old cellar and boiler room have been excavated to a depth of about six feet.

Permission for the dig was granted by the Diocese of Manchester and the city council, who will be turning the over-grown and vandalised graveyard into a public garden. "We have started our dig now because just recently there have been more urgent talks than ever about the council turning the graveyard into a park," said Mr Bateman. "Obviously, it would be too late to do anything once they start work on that".

He recently took two weeks holiday to work on the dig, with members of STAG joining him at weekends and although the weather has hardly helped things along, quite a lot of work has been done.

"There is a large area to excavate but we hope to finish our work by Christmas," said Mr Bateman. The group will continue into the New Year if the council is not ready to start work on its own scheme by then.

Up to date, the most common find has been coke! — When the church was demolished in 1949 the cellar contained a fair quantity of the fuel for the boiler — but several large chunks of masonry have been unearthed.

HALF-TIMBERED

The first St Clement's Church of which there is any record was built in 1512 and this is the one STAG are looking for. It served as a chapel-of-ease to the parish of Manchester. It was built in the half-timbered style and replaced by a plain brick building when it was taken down in 1779.

The new building only comprised a narrow nave and a small apse and was fitted with high oak pews. "When they rebuilt it in 1780, they built a brick church of the same size but Chorlton's population was beginning to grow so in 1837 the north and south walls were removed and two aisles added," said Mr Bateman.

Not until 1850 was Chorlton constituted as a separate ecclesiastical parish with the dean and canons of the cathedral as patrons.

Although they are not expecting to find any buried treasure, STAG members have recovered many pieces of "foggy" glass which could be from the 1512 church. "The pieces look very old and may well be from the first church but it is difficult to say right now," said Mr Bateman.

Regulars at the neighbouring Bowling Green public house often pass comment when they see the group digging away within the cemetery walls. STAG will not be disturbing any graves though and are working under the watchful eye of the Greater Manchester Archaeological Unit.

INTEREST

Indeed, it is the regulars of the Bowling Green Hotel who may benefit from anything STAG does find as Mr Bateman explained. "The pub is to be refurbished and the architect expressed an interest in some of the objects which he would like to incorporate into the decor".

"The Bowling Green pub has been there since about 1693 when it may well have been called the Church Inn so it is very appropriate that something from the old church should be included in the new decor," he said.

When the dig is completed, details will be published of the work and discoveries made. "An archaeological dig is not just for the benefit of the people who do it and there will be a record for other people to refer too," he said.

The publication is likely to prove popular reading — people from as far away as Bramhall have shown their interest and willingness to help with the dig.

When it is all over and the council turn it into a public garden, Mr Bateman hopes that the cemetery will be regarded as respectable enough to bring back the headstone which used to mark the grave of PC Nicholas Cock who was murdered by Charles Peace, a burglar. The headstone was removed to Preston Police

Searching for the 16th century St Clement's 1981

1 Bateman, Angus J., Excavations and Other Investigations at Old St Clements Church Yard Chorlton Manchester 1977, Report of work done in part fulfilment of the Certificate Course in Methods of Archaeology, Extra-mural Department, University of Manchester, held by South Trafford Archaeological Group, Page 1
2 South Trafford Archaeological Group

Liverpool half penny

earliest coin was a silver half groat dating from Charles I, which was found alongside pennies dating from 1797 and 1863. These pennies are notable in their own way. The 18th century Cartwheel penny was the first serious attempt by the Government to produce low denominational coinage, while the 1863 Bun penny represents the switch from copper to bronze.

But it is the Liverpool halfpenny which reveals more about the life of ordinary people, because this coin was not issued by the Government, but by an individual, and highlights the real problem that many people had in obtaining low denominational coinage. Even before the Middle Ages there were just not enough coins that could be used for day to day business.

This was partly addressed in the 17th century, when private individuals began issuing tokens, usually as a mixture of half pennies and farthings, and were redeemable at the place of business of the issuer. This rather tied the individual to trading with the businessman who issued the tokens and were perhaps not so useful to people living in rural areas, because most were issued from towns and cities. During the 17th century, there were fifteen issues from Manchester, twelve from Liverpool, seventeen from Warrington, nine from Preston and more from some of the smaller Lancashire towns.[1] A second large issue of tokens across Lancashire began sometime between 1783 and 1785.

Our coin was issued in 1791 in Liverpool as part of a very large series by Thomas Clarke, who produced ten tons of these copper coins between 1791 and '94. Clarke was a Liverpool merchant, and his coins could only be redeemable at his warehouse in Liverpool.[2] The coin itself, although common, remains a beautiful piece of work. The obverse side shows a ship under canvas with crossed laurel branches beneath, and the inscription "Liverpool Half penny". The reverse bears the motto and arms of Liverpool. Ours had not fared so well, and part of upper mast and rigging from the ship had worn away.

Manchester followed with its own coins from 1792, and these were produced by John Fielding, who was a grocer and tea dealer, and may have had a warehouse at 12 Back Falkner Street or 27 Withy Grove. His earlier coins bore the Grocers' Arms and a detail of the East India House, which was later replaced by the bale mark used by the East India Company to identify its various cargoes. His second issue showed a porter bowed down with the weight of a bale on one side, and the words "Success to Navigation", which was a reference to Duke's Canal.[3] These were redeemable at his warehouse.

A third set of Manchester tokens were issued in 1793 by a J. Rayner & Company, but within four years all of these tokens were made obsolete by the issue of copper coinage by the Government. These were from Mathew Boulton's Soho Mint in Birmingham, and included our cartwheel penny along with two pennies, half pennies and farthings.

During the dig 1981

1 The Ormskirk & West Lancashire Numismatic Society, www.numsoc.net
2 Thomas Clarke was a grocer living at 12 Cable Street and had a warehouse at no 4 Marshall Street off Lord Street.
3 Ibid, The Ormskirk & West Lancashire Numismatic Society

Painstaking work at the dig 1981

The discovery of one Liverpool half penny in itself does not throw much light on the working of the local economy, and it may just casually have found its way into the township more as a curiosity than a means of exchange. But if it was in use as a substitute coin, then it raises questions about how it was used. Given that it was redeemable in Liverpool and that similar tokens were circulating in Manchester, was there an interchange of tokens between these companies, so could a Liverpool half penny be exchanged in Manchester? And if so, was there a trade in the tokens between small businesses, allowing, for instance, someone to exchange their token in a local shop, which would then redeem them at the issuing warehouse? This ad hoc arrangement would seem to be a practical response to trading with a city based warehouse.

Of course this 1791 half penny really sits outside our story. If it had been circulating as a means of exchange by the 1840s, it would be just an interesting relic, and already beyond the memory of most in the township.

The Queen Victoria medallion however would be the stuff of recent history. Victoria had been crowned in 1837, and the medallion commemorated the coronation. It was a yellow metal medallion, 23mm in diameter and less than 1 mm thick. A hole had been drilled so that it could be hung around the neck, or perhaps even as part of a wrist band. On the obverse was a profile of the young Queen in the centre, and the inscription "*Her Gracious Majesty Victoria*" around the edge. In the centre of the reverse side was a Crown the inscription "*Born May 24 1819*" above, and "*Crowned June 28 1838*" below.

There was also a 9ct gold ring which belonged to a child. This, like all the finds had been lost when they fell through the floor of the church onto the sandy surface below. All were found in one of the side aisles, which date their loss to after 1837, that, being the year the aisles were added to the church.

Now, while finds like these are at the core of any dig, it was the unexpected skeletons which proved both disturbing to the team and the closest link with the people of the township. They were all found underneath the north aisle, but had been buried before the extension of the church in 1837.

In one case the excavation revealed a foot, leg and shroud pin, which was made of "heavily tinned cooper wire". And with his usual attention to detail Angus had taken the bones home,

Old St Clements Circa 1512

St Clement's 1512

St Clement's churchyard 1978

"cleaned them and reassembled them, with the help of Gray's Anatomy", a task he admitted *"was very tricky for an amateur"*.[1]

But it was the complete undisturbed skeleton of a new born child which most affected members of the team. Even today thirty years on, something of the drama and sadness of the discovery is revealed from the report, *"It was found right against the 1780 wall at a depth of 70 cm. Every tiny bone I could see was collected, washed and taken home for analysis. I was impressed by the perfect condition of these bones when compared with the adult leg bones... Because of the immature ossification, each vertebra was in 3 pieces, and the skull disarticulated into many separate bones. The cranial bones were the only damaged ones, presumably crushed by the collapsing coffin. They were paper thin"*.[2]

That evening, the skull of an adult taken to be the mother, was unearthed beside the child. Its teeth were in perfect condition, which led Angus to assume it was a young woman, but the documentary evidence was less conclusive. The only mother and child recorded fitting the grave position were Mary Lamb and her daughter Betty. They were buried in 1778 and, while Betty fitted the profile, having died aged 7 days, Mary was 44 which seemed too old for the skull. If it is their grave, then the human tragedy is all the more profound. Young Betty died on April 6th and her mother three days later on the 9th. And in the years stretching back to 1760, Mary and her husband had already buried five other children.

Less gruesome but no less important was the discovery of a large collection of window glass and painted plaster, which was compared with examples in the new church and elsewhere. No conclusive date was possible for the window glass, but expert advice suggested a date in the 1860s, although it is possible some could have been early 19th century. A later date may fit with the improvements funded by William Cunliffe Brooks, who remained a supporter of the old church long after the new one had been built on Edge Lane. And it is possible that some of the glass might be from the large east window which Cunliffe Brooks donated.

The dig was supported where possible with oral testimony of people who knew the old church before it was demolished. They confirmed that it was still lit by oil lamps before the First World War, and had painted plastered walls. One of those interviewed was able to identify what may have been part of the lectern.[3]

Window fragments, St Clement's 19th century

1 Ibid, Bateman 1977 Report Page 9
2 Ibid, Bateman 1977 Report Page 10
3 Ibid, Simpson, Andrew, pages 272-279

Chorlton Row, the lane out of the village...

a few posh houses, a blacksmith, two farmers and a collection of wattle and daub cottages with a pond and a mystery all thrown in.

Now it may be stretching it to describe Beech Road as the lane half as old as time, but it is old, and I suspect it will have been used long before Henry VIII married Anne Boleyn, and perhaps even before Alfred burnt his cakes.

It was the main route from Barlow Moor Lane down to the village Green, and was one of the three ways in and out of Chorlton.[1]

Brownhill's Cottage circa 1900

Beech Road 1933

1 The others were the lane that ran from the green past the Horse and Jockey, across Edge Lane and running then as Manchester Road to West Point, and the lane that ran out to Turn Moss and one to Stretford.

Beech Road from Barlow Moor Road 1959

And it still retains an echo of its earlier existence, which is best seen on an early summer's morning, before even the milkman has started his round, when you can get a clear view

Beech Road 1975

34

Beech Road 1910

of how it twists and turns to accommodate obstacles which have long since vanished.

Beech Road 1975

35

Mr Sharp's superior house...
being a catalogue of some odd goings on, more than a few rum things, and the sudden end of that superior building.

   Mr Sharp's fine house stood back from the lane and was sandwiched between the old Wesleyan Chapel on one side, and the smithy of Mr William Davis on the other and long after the chapel had become a furniture warehouse and the smithy ceased its magic business of heating and hammering, Mr Sharp's house stood firm.

Mr Sharp's former home 2012

    By then it was in need of much tender care, and had acquired an extension which jutted out from the building, but something of its former elegance remained.

    Like so many of our early 19th century buildings, after much neglect including two fires, it was demolished in 2016, leaving a hole in the ground which has yet to be filled, and a fascinating story.

    Once it was home to Daniel Sharp, who lived here certainly from 1841 and maybe earlier.

    He was a wine merchant, and may have moved into the property with his new wife, after their marriage in 1833.

    Sadly, she died in 1846 leaving him a widow. I say widow, but there is the interesting little interlude of a second marriage

Mr Sharp's former home 1976

in 1852, when he married his servant Ann Bailey, who was much younger than him.

The marriage seemed not to be successful, for nine years later, she is no longer with him, and in his will made shortly before he died having left her nothing, he adds a codicil and awards her a small sum of money.

The house has had a varied set of occupants, since then gaining an extension sometime between 1894 and 1907 but by the end of the last century it was empty and sliding into dereliction, leaving me only to report one last episode in its history. One night sometime in the mid 1980s, we were walking past the place and noticed signs that advertised the grounds as a car park, which, according to my friend, was all very irregular, as there had been no planning permission granted for such use.

It was perhaps fortunate that before any of us could raise the issue with the Corporation, we noticed that the firm was based in London, and the vehicles parked up consisted of a London black cab and a London Transport bus. Had we looked a little closer at the signboard above the entrance to the brick extension, we might have recognised the name Bulman, and made the link with a television drama. And had we then turned up in the morning, we would have seen the TV crew and actors.

Such today is Beech Road that it regularly features in television dramas, and was the backdrop for the film, "Looking for Eric", which provided gainful employment for some of our residents.

Mr Sharp's former home 2013

Etchells and the Beech Road Takeaway...
a century and more of newspapers, sweets and battered cod and chips.

There will be those who might question the addition of the newsagents and chippy, but they have more than a claim to be admitted to the Chorlton Hall of Fame, for both have traded continuously as such since the properties were built at the beginning of the last century.

During its long history of serving up battered cod and chips, the chippy has had many names, but my favourite has to be when it was known affectionately as the "Vimto Chippy, because of the Vimto stickers around the edge of the window.

And that newsagents on the corner of Beech Road and Chequers Road has more than a passing link to much of our earlier history, for it was here that Mr Nixon sold his papers and confectionery,

Mr and Mrs Nixon 1939

40

just a short walk from where his grandparents' parents had run the Travellers Rest from the 1840s, and his great grandfather had dispensed pints from the pub over the water, which everyone now knows as Jackson's Boat, but was once the Greyhound.

Nor does the history stop there because Mr Nixon had married a Miss Brownhill, whose grandfather had been the village wheelwright, and had a side trade in selling beer, along with renting out cottages on Sandy Lane, which were, of course, known as Brownhill's Buildings.

All of which is a bit of a walk from Mr Nixon's shop, which in its time also stretched to lending out books. Many of our newsagents broadened out to lending books, and Ida Bradshaw remembers, "It was all fiction and you could only borrow one book at time, but could change books several times in one week. From what I recall quite a lot of newsagents had them - mainly for people who didn't belong to the council library".

The newsagents 1958

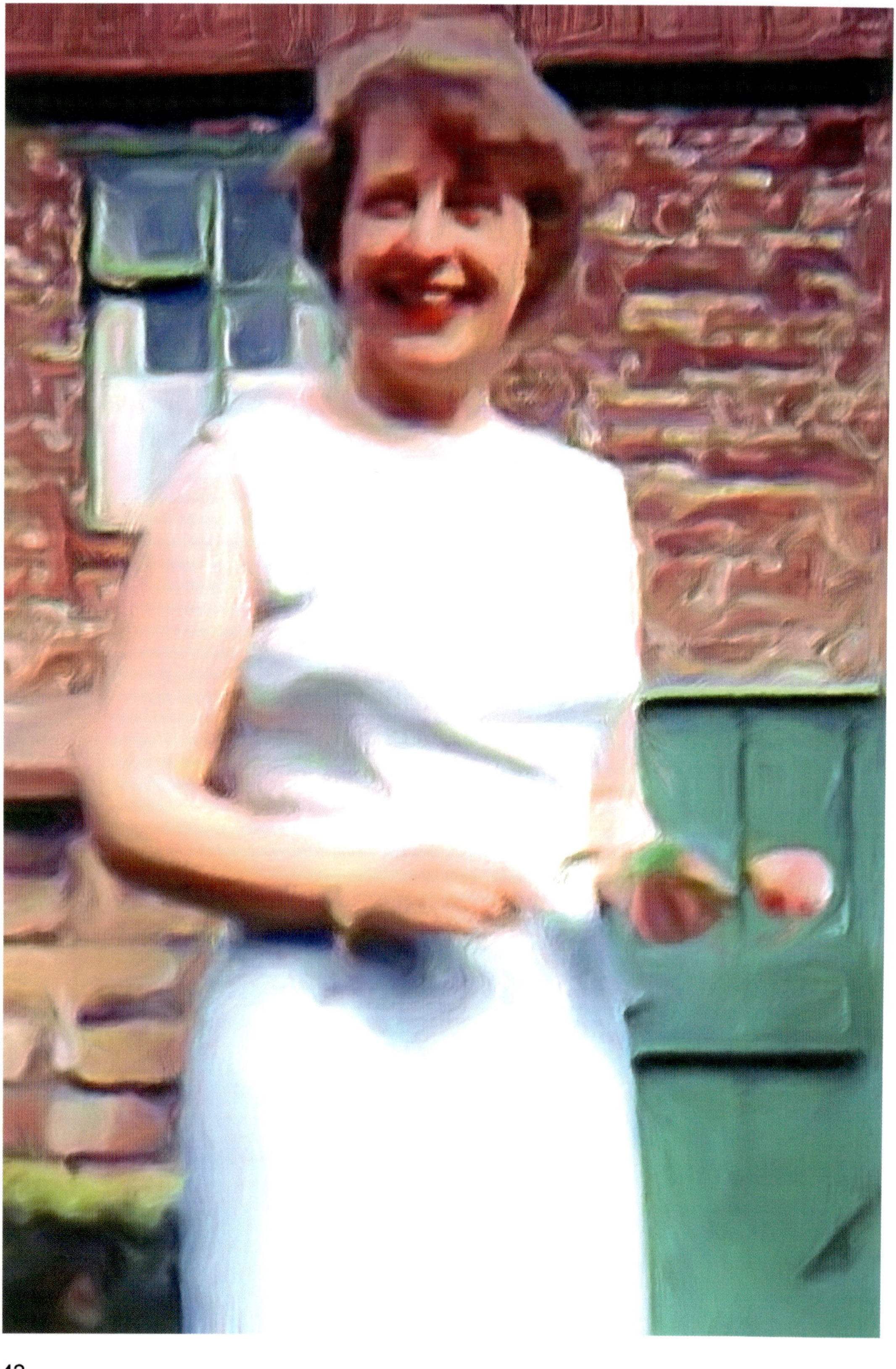

Marjorie Holmes 1921-2014...

a dear friend and a guardian of our history.

Marjorie Holmes was born in Chorlton and, apart from her war service, lived all her life around the old village.

Her dad had a workshop in the yard of the old farmhouse on the Green, which is now Finney Drive, and the family possessed one of those old fabulous looking cars.

Majorie Holmes and mother 1928

She was an accomplished artist and had a wealth of stories of when, according to her, Chorlton was "still Chorlton".

I never quite understood what she meant by that, but hers had been a childhood when the last vestiges of the old rural Chorlton were just passing away, and she could talk about that period with great authority.

She had played on the meadows when it was still farmland, remembered going to the local farm for milk and was firmly of the opinion that, "them in New Chorlton were a snooty lot who were all fancy cakes and silk knickers", and if she wanted to be particularly dismissive she added, "all fancy cakes and no knickers".

Dear Andy,

Well you did ask! So don't blame me if I have burdened you with more information than you really wanted. What started off as scraps of notes took me over and snowballed. and I must admit I've thoroughly enjoyed myself without having to move much further than my armchair.

Majorie's introduction to her story 2000

Jasmine Cottage Marjorie Holmes date unknown

Of course I could never really be sure that underneath her bold sweeping statements there was not more than a little mischief.

I must have spent hours sitting in her back room on Provis Road, listening to all the tales about her frequent late attendance at school, the times when she had stopped to watch Mr Clark the blacksmith carrying out his magic of "heating and hammering", or sitting in the cellar of the family home on Stockton Road during the Manchester Blitz.

Much of what she remembered she committed to paper, including a vivid account I still have of Beech Road in the early 1930s.

"The wine and spirit shop at the corner of Chequers Road was Mason and Burroughs.

In that row there was a bakers and a provision shop where, in the 1930s I would be sent for 1d. worth of balm (yeast) for my mother to make bread. In those days we had a black leaded grate with a coal-fired oven.

Oh the joy of returning home from school to the aroma of homemade bread, and a specially made little cob, still warm from the oven and spread with butter.

There was also a good hardware shop, Harris's, where one could buy anything from screws and pot hooks, to donkey stone, which was to cream our steps, along with brushes, buckets and dolly tubs.

The end shop before the passage was Rowley's Butchers, who always had sawdust on the floor. This, I suppose, soaked up any blood from carcasses hung up on hooks and was easy to sweep up.

Across the passage, where the Italian shop is situated [now

San Juan], was Hyde's outdoor license. I think they only sold beer. We could go there with a jug to purchase beer, which was hand pumped, to take home.

There is a passage at the back of this row of shops leading to the stables, where Hydes's stables are to be seen on Acres Road.

Acres Road was commonly called the Crack. Down the passage, against the drainpipe is a roughly chiselled out commemoration of a faithful dog.

I cannot recall the use of the shop previous to Richard and Muriel's [now Sherlock Holmes], but the corner shop, now a restaurant, was a hairdresser's (ladies), and prior to that - pre-war - a cycle shop Cavanaugh's (the name maybe spelled wrongly) and cycle repair shop.

Across Acres Road was the Grange laundry where, when they became mechanised with delivery vans, old Mr Greaves was allowed to continue delivering laundry in his horse-drawn van.

Then there was Lister's sweet shop, opposite the blacksmiths. Mrs Lister used to frighten children.

The rest of the block was the Co-op stores. The first part led to the stables and delivery yard. The rest of the block was the grocers, where several assistants were employed. There was a lady who sat in an elevated box.

She was the cashier. The grocers sent the money and grocery list in a metal can which was attached to a pulley and sent across a wire, where she would check the list and send back the receipt and change.

I think there were two of these, one at each end of the shop.

There had been grocers on the corner before the Co-op.

The Co-op butchers were round the corner on Stockton Road".

Marjorie's dad Higson Avenue 1930

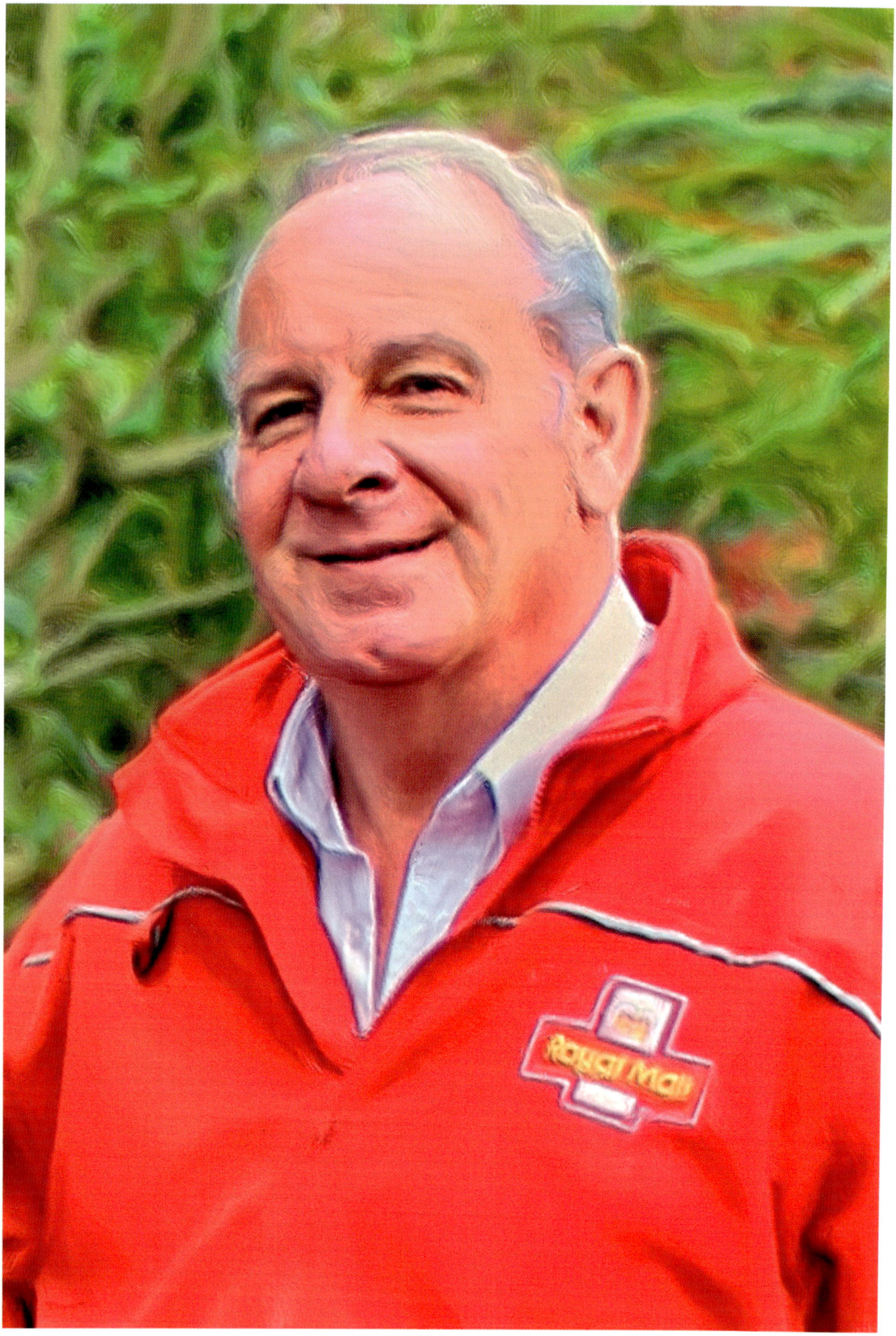
Royal Mail

David's shop circa 1979

The Living Legend that is Dave the Butcher...

"It has been an honour and a privilege to serve and work with the people of Chorlton-cum-Hardy for over 45 years".[1]

Mention the name Dave the Butcher and it is odds on that people will smile, recount a story about his shop, or an equally fond memory of a conversation with him at the parcels counter of Chorlton Post Office.

So that was enough to induct him into the Hall of Fame, and what better way to tell his story than in his own words.

"My family's grandparents lived in Chorlton and I was born in Chequers Road, and sixty-five years later I am living on Beaumont Road, which is not very far from where I started life.

I moved into to 36 Beech Road and ran it as a butcher's shop when I was just 20 in 1972, and still to this day I get the name 'Dave the Butcher'.

David the postman

1 In conversation with David Wilkinson, September 27, 2017

47

David's children in the shop

My customers were wonderful, and I continued as a butcher for nearly twenty-five years. It was in the family with Dad, my uncle and three brothers all having butcher's shops. Christmas was magical, and my wife of forty years helped me decorate the shop, especially for the children who came into the shop with their mums and dad.

I have many stories to tell but will share just two.

A lady well into her 80s who was a good friend as well as a customer had frequent black outs. She was very scared of going into hospital and made me promise her that if it ever happened in my shop, I was not to get an ambulance to send her to hospital. I agreed but did tell her if she was hurt or very poorly I would do the right thing and send for help. It happened and bless her, she had a bad turn. I didn't want everyone to see her so distressed so I calmly lifted her up over my shoulder, giving her a fireman's lift and placed her on my bed upstairs. After ten minutes she came round and I made her a cup of tea with sugar, then put her in my car and took her home. She lived nearly another ten years after the incident and we always laughed about what happened.

The second story was of a lady called Celia living in Chorltonville. She was a very kind and eccentric lady, who looked after animals including dogs and twelve cats. I saw photographs in her house of squirrel monkeys hanging from the picture rails in her lounge and of other squirrel monkeys in cages in her back garden.

Celia told me she was bitten by a monkey, which caused a thrombosis. The monkeys were taken to Chester Zoo.

One evening I called to her house with an order of meat for the animals.

David's early career as a postman

She asked me would I look at Bobby, her black Labrador as she said he was not well. On looking at him I noticed he was stiff and had probably been dead for several days. She asked me to bury the dog for her in the back garden. Having then dug the hole in the pouring rain she changed her mind and wanted him in the front garden. After a short prayer and chosen words, I buried Billy. Three days later on a Saturday morning when the shop was packed Celia asked loudly 'Did I tell you Billy died". To which I replied 'I hope so, I buried him in your front garden three days ago.'

After nearly twenty-five years as a butcher I sold my shop and changed jobs.

I had applied and successfully passed to join both the Police Force and the Royal Mail, but the Post Office won out and I worked first as a postman, and then inside the delivery office for over 20 years, during which time I met many customers who became friends, from footballers Denis Law, Wyn Davies and many Coronation Street stars , like Alison King, Vicky Binns, Chris Quentine, Sarah Louise Platt and Kevin Kennedy, and the wonderful Eddie Yates and our own Chef, Simon Rimmer.

When I retired I got many warm messages on Facebook, and I thank everyone in Chorlton.

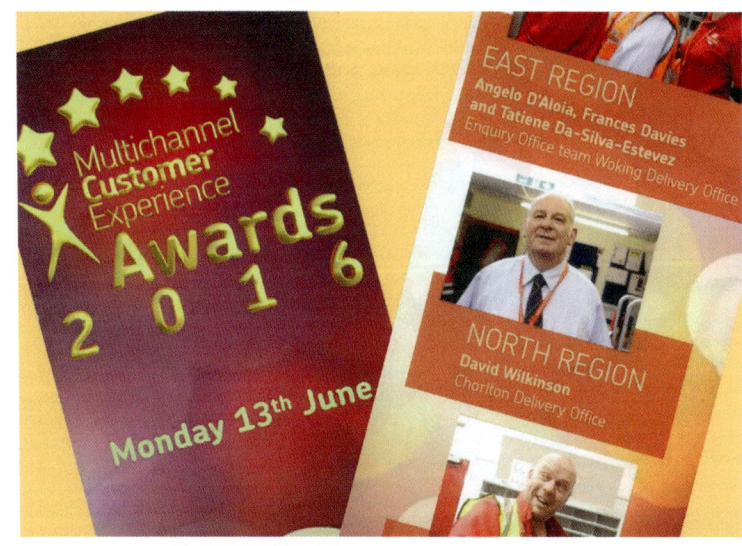

Recognising David's contribution, his award 2016

Sutton's Cottage...
thatched roof, wood and plaster walls and a garden whose secrets are still there to see.

Now I doubt that anyone who visited Dave the butcher's shop will have realized that they were just a short walk from Sutton's Cottage, which stood on the site of the Laundrette from sometime in the 1780s, through till 1894.

It was a wattle and daub cottage and in the 1840s there may still have been upwards of fifty of them in Chorlton.

They were constructed from a timber framework, with walls made of branches woven together and covered with a mixture of clay, gravel, hay and even horse hair, and topped with a thatched roof.

And from the 1840s, for over half a century our cottage was the home of Samuel and Sarah Sutton and their two children.

One photograph still exists of the cottage, and it shows white walls and wooden beams partly obscured by ivy. The front door was approached through a small country garden, and behind the house and, away from the view of strangers, stood the privy and the back garden, where the Sutton's grew fruit, vegetables and flowers. There would be currant and gooseberry bushes, raspberry canes, rhubarb and mix of vegetables, which made an important contribution to the family income, and were often home to chickens and even a pig.

Such houses were easy to build and equally easy to maintain, but there could be disadvantages to living in them. The porous nature of walls meant they were damp, and crumbling clay meant endless repairs.

Mr Sutton was a farm labourer, and long after his death his wife Sarah continued to live in the cottage until she died in 1892.

32-38 Beech Road 1958

Sutton's Cottages circa 1885

Beech House...
that big pile of a place at the top of the Row, its illustrious owners the Holt family, and a bit on Malton Avenue, which was once where Mr Holt admired his roses.

Now I doubt that anyone waiting for a bus in the old tram terminus on Barlow Moor Road will be aware that, once, standing by the Diving Club building, would have made them liable for trespass. Moreover, their view of the road would have been obscured by a very tall brick wall, because this was the eastern bit of Mr Holt's garden, and had been since the 1830s.

The garden stretched along Beech Road, from a little past Cross Road, up to Barlow Moor Road and all the way to High Lane, and then back down High Lane, almost to Cross Road.

In the centre of this large garden was their home, which looked to have been an impressive building. From the upstairs windows, the family had commanding views south, towards Chorlton Brook and the Mersey, and east across fields they owned, to Hough End Hall.

They had made their money in the manufacture of the wooden blocks used for calico engraving, and their 18th century town house was the double fronted property on the southern side of St John Street, which still stands today.

They also owned an extensive portfolio of properties around St John Street, as well as land in Chorlton.

Three generations of the Holt family had lived there, but the last had died in 1906, and by 1908 the house was empty and the estate was awaiting sale. By sheer chance a postcard showing the lodge has survived.

The message records a pleasant afternoon spent in the grounds, and the speculation that it was soon to disappear. "Edith and I had tea on the lawn of the big house, which you see is the lodge in the picture. It will soon be sold and then will probably be divided into small plots".

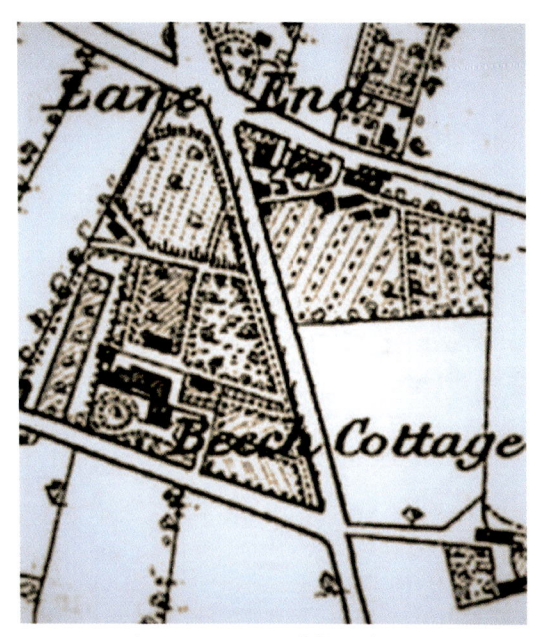

By the following year, the part of the garden which ran the length of Barlow Moor Road as far as High Lane had been bought by Manchester Corporation, who felled the trees, demolished the wall, and built the tram terminus on the land.

Later renamed Beech House 1854

The remaining land was developed with the cinema and a row of shops, and the garage of Mr Shaw, along with Malton Avenue.

Residents of the avenue have, over the years, come across what were parts of the original paths for the garden of Beech House, and bits of the original brick boundary wall can still be seen.

All of which brings us almost to the edge of the old village. North will take us to the Four Banks and New Chorlton, while a slight detour along Claude Road will end at Chorltonville, which is where we are bound next.

Barlow Moor Road, Beech Road 1907

53

CHORLTONVILLE
And the Estate to the east.

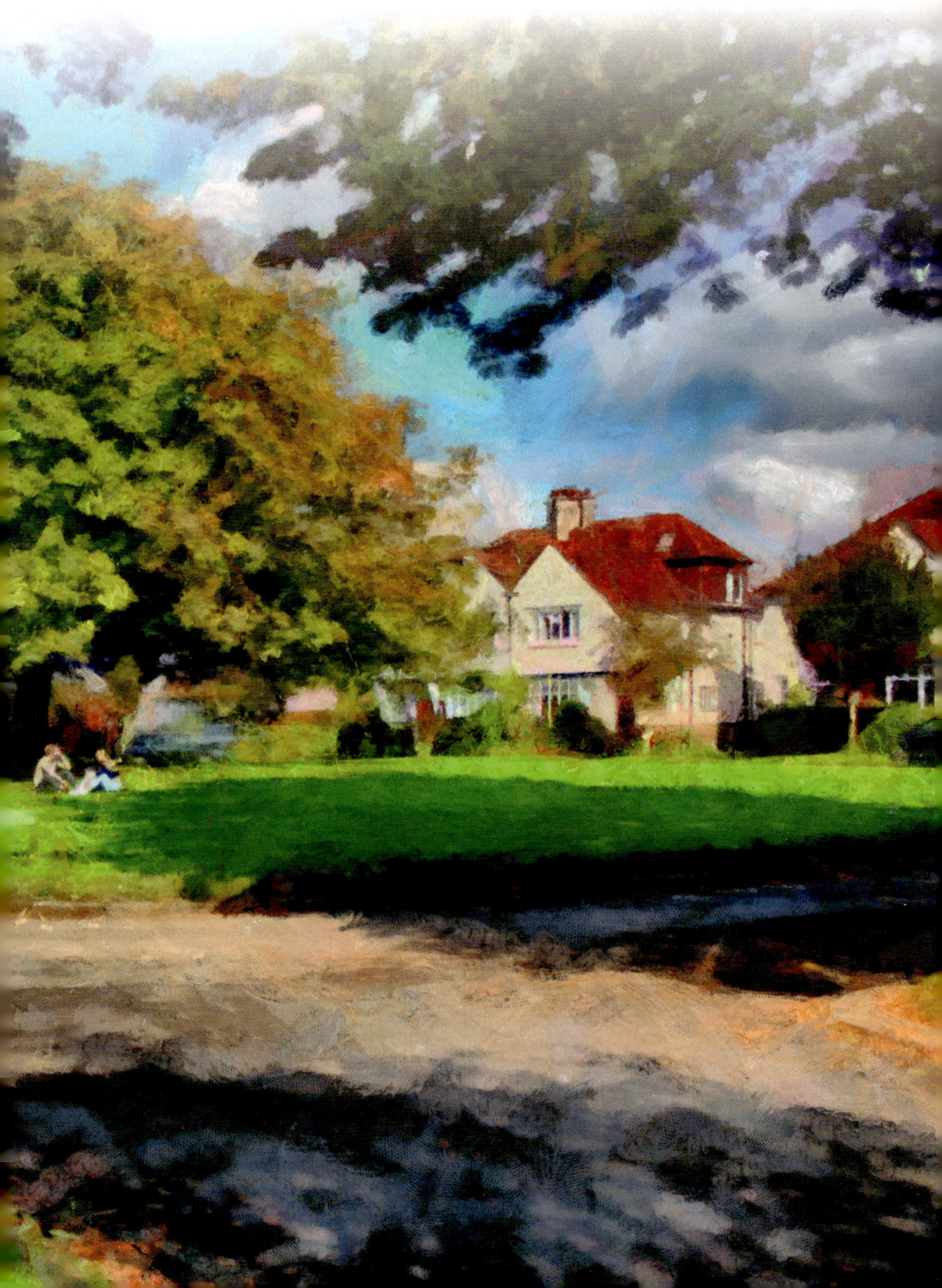

Chorltonville and the Estate to the east

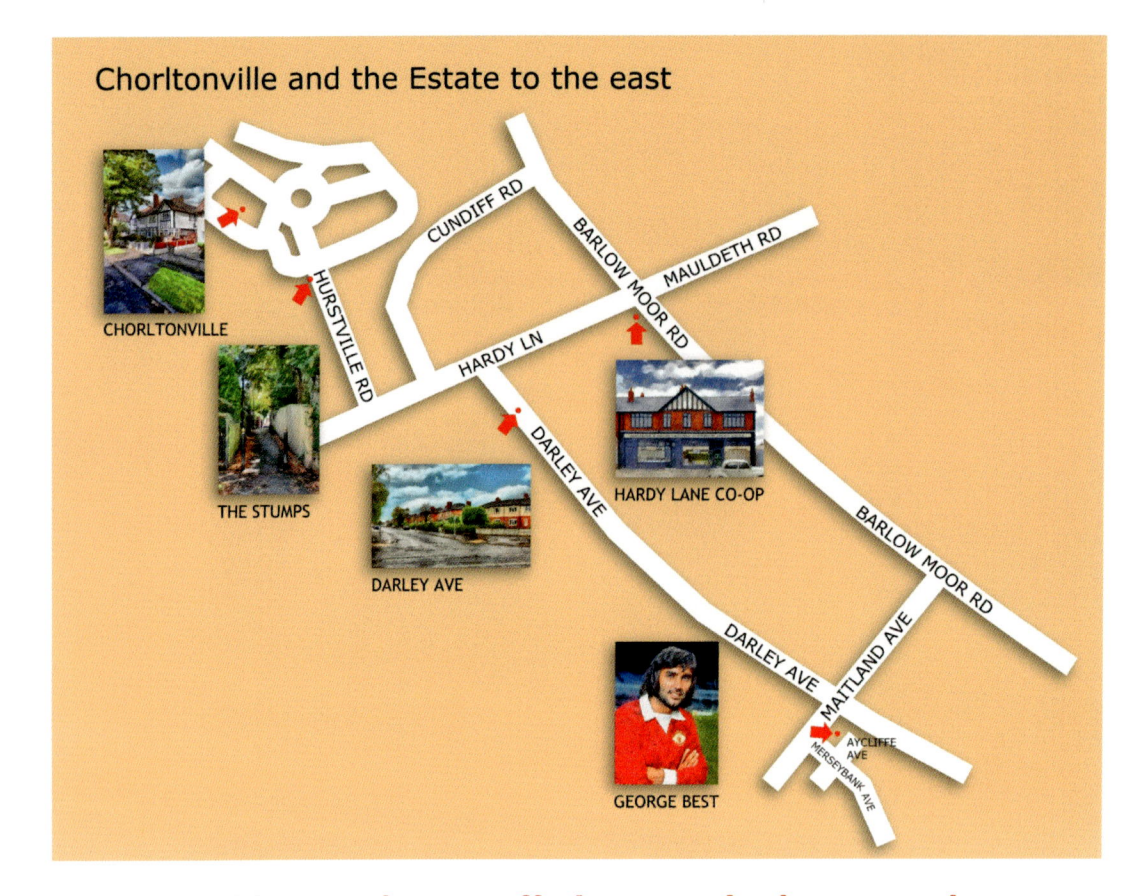

Bold new schemes offering superior homes at decent rents, comprising Chorltonville, the Cundiff Road Estate and Darley Avenue.

Now it may seem odd to group Chorltonville, and the Cundiff Road, and the Darley Avenue Estates together but they were all bold schemes to provide superior homes at affordable rents.

Chorltonville dates from 1911 while Cundiff, Darley and Mersey Bank are later. All have fairly well defined boundaries and all have matured over the century or so since they were built.

Of the three, the "Ville" remains pretty much an island with just three ways in. For those with a sense of history the route from the Brookburn Bridge up past the school follows an old footpath, which meanders through the estate before exiting at the Stumps, and moving on along what is now Hurstville Road to Hardy Lane. Those choosing this path will be able to tick off two of the ways in and out, leaving only Claude Road, which

Claude Road circa 1907

travels south from Beech Road before gently curving to join Reynard Road, and thence continuing as Claude Road into the "Ville".

The Naked Civil Servant 1968

But before dismissing Claude Road as just a way into Chorltonville, it is worth noting that it was here that Quentin Crisp died while visiting a friend, on the eve of a national revival of his one man show in 1999. The event was of course covered by the media, including a short article by David McKie which reflected on attractions of Chorlton, and made mention of the "sturdy Safeways, and several restaurants and bars and endless supplies of buses", before describing Beech Road and

57

Steve Pullen with the Great Britain Visually Impaired Judo Squad and Coaches 2002

concluding with Chorltonville, the water park and golf course.[1]

It is a slightly flippant description, but one that, while it is now frozen in time, will interest anyone who remembers the Soap Opera, Bryan the Book and the Trevor Arms when the pub still claimed to be the "Famous Trevor Arms".

And that nicely brings me to Steve Pullen MBE, who lives on Claude Road in one of those houses which look like they should be in the "Ville", and which, according to Steve, should

Churchill Fellowship Award 1989 presented by Her Majesty the Queen

be, given that they were built by the same company in advance of the estate being constructed. His house also has that rare feature of a post box set into the side wall of the garden, which some might argue qualifies it as unusual.

Steve is better known for being a key figure in the development of judo in the region. In a long sporting career which has encompassed rugby, wrestling, sambo wrestling and boxing as well as judo, he has achieved a succession of awards and honours. These have included, the Churchill Fellowship Award 1989 presented by Her Majesty the Queen. Coach of the Year for 1991 and '94, induction into the Coaching Hall of Fame, and his award of an MBE for his services to visually impaired and disabled judo. But I suspect he may well be proudest of those awards, and thank you letters, which have come for his work in coaching disadvantaged children, along with his role in the Olympic Games including "his commitment and contribution to the success of the Sydney 2000 Paralympic Games".[2]

Nor does it stop there because he has recently attained the level of 7th Dan Black Belt, which is a supreme achievement in the world of judo.

Chorltonville from the air 1925

[1] I wouldn't be seen dead dying there, the Manchester Guardian, November 25, 1999
[2] Citation on the 2000 Paralympic Games certificate

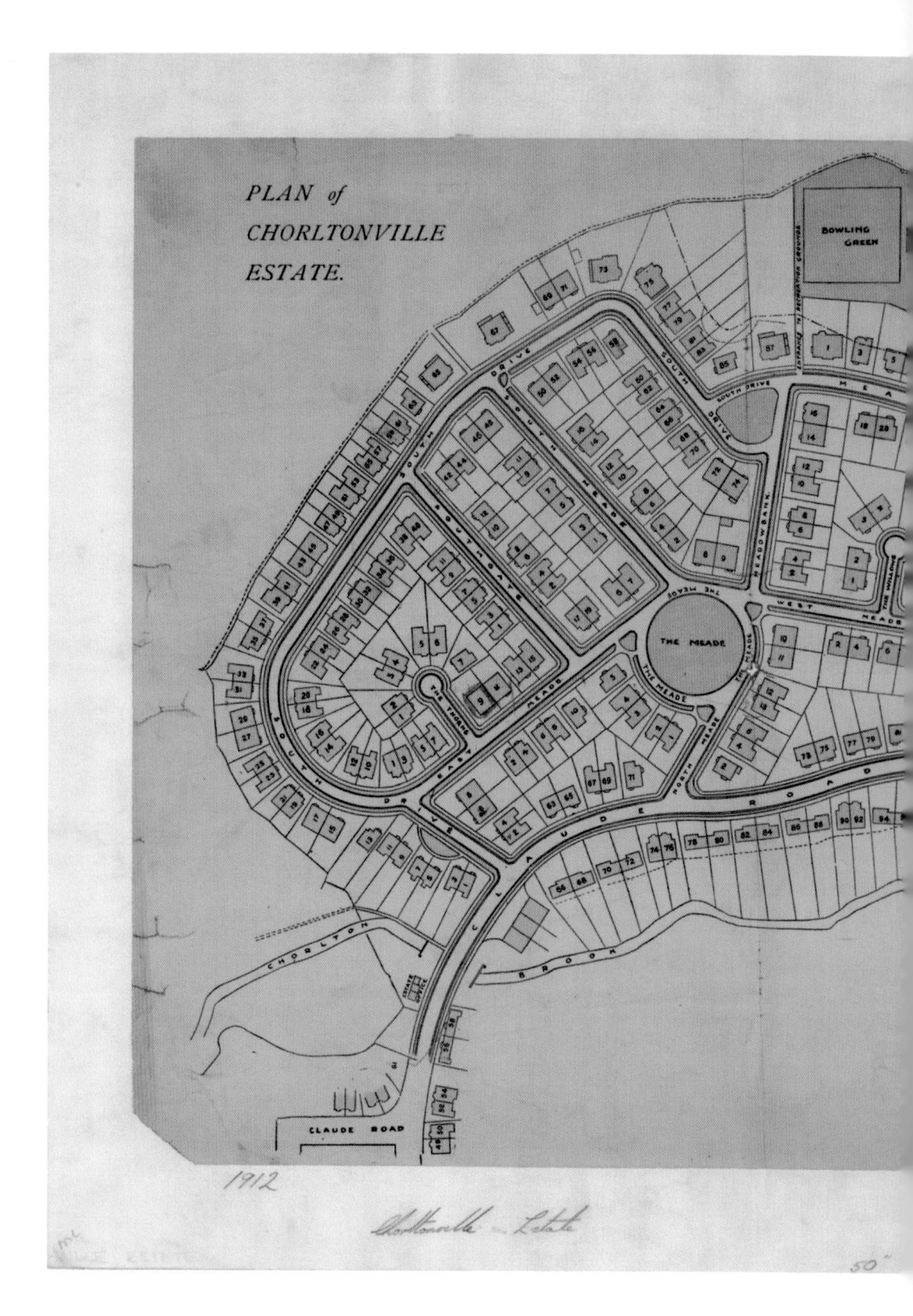

PLAN of CHORLTONVILLE ESTATE.

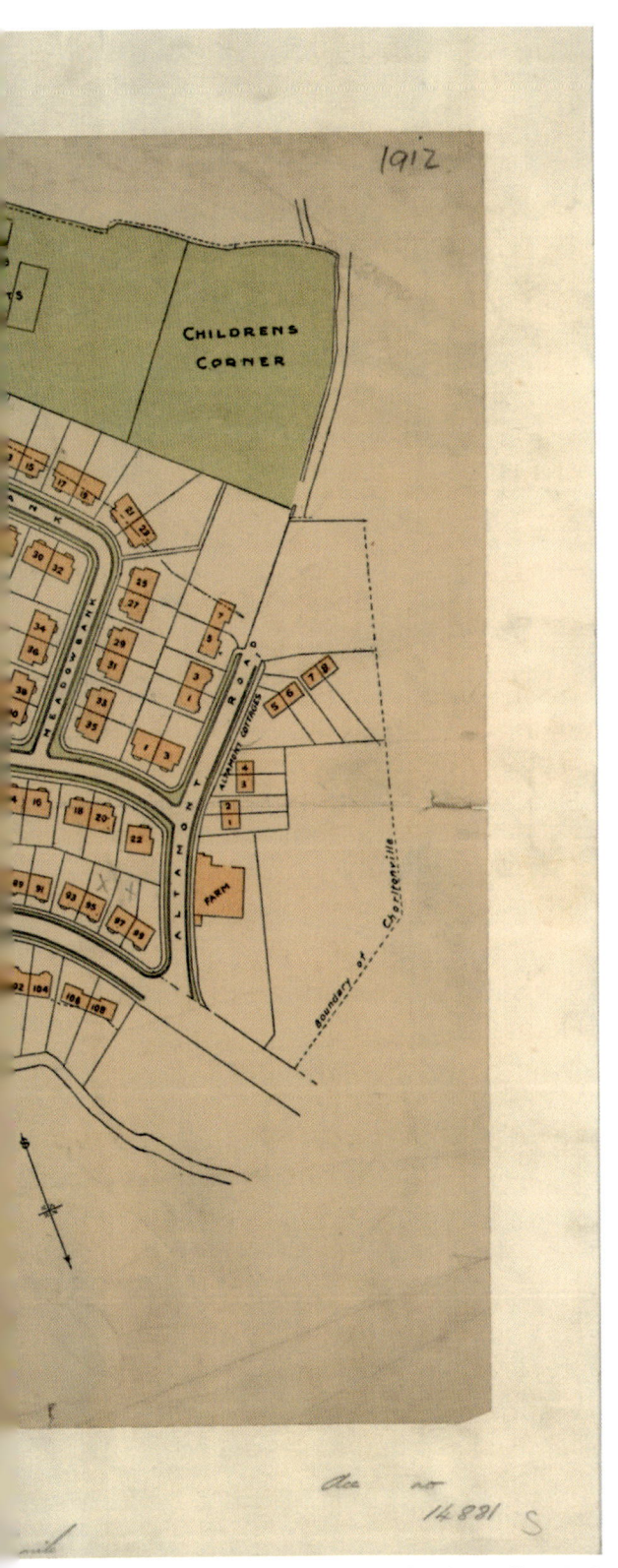

Chorltonville 1912

Chorltonville...

"the curved roads and the houses of various designs in black and white make one feel almost that one was living in Elizabethan times".

Now the story of the "Ville" is pretty well known, and in essence is the story of a scheme to offer homes at affordable prices, on what was still the edge of the countryside.

The properties, "were let at rentals of £24 a year and

CHORLTONVILLE

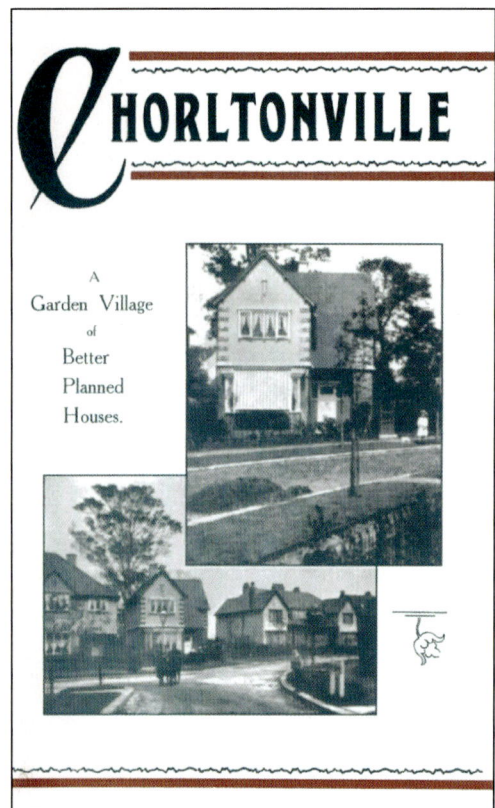

A Garden Village of Better Planned Houses.

Welcome to Chorltonville 1912

upwards and each tenant was a shareholder", and building was completed within two years.[1]

A whole raft of civic dignitaries had been invited to the opening day on October 7 1911, and one of those who spoke was our own Mrs Jane Redford, who was the first woman councillor elected in Chorlton.

She commented that the estate was "far removed from what was described as 'brick boxes with slate lids', and as to the inside, she was pleased to know that the rooms were bright, airy, and well ventilated, and provided with electric light (or gas if desired), and with gas for stoves and wash boilers".[2]

All of which offers up one of those bizarre episodes where the

Open day in Chorltonville 1911

Gas Department of Manchester Corporation was in direct competition with the Electric Department, who not only engaged in undercutting the price offered by the Gas Department, but, in the case of Chorltonville, actually undertook "only to supply each house with electric current provided there was no gas in the house at all for lighting".[3]

It was, however, a dispute which was settled with a compromise of gas downstairs and electricity upstairs, which was just a little less bizarre than the fact that there are no telephone poles, unlike other parts of Chorlton, with the GPO completing the wiring underground.[4]

That said, what exercised the directors of the estate and made them unhappy, were "Chorlton Brook and the sewage farm nearby", and they made the request that the "sewage farm should not be enlarged, but if possible be curtailed".

It was a request which was politely ignored.

1 Mr J.H. Dawson, Chorltonville, Opening of a New Garden Suburb, Manchester Guardian, October 9, 1911.
2 Mrs J. Redford, ibid, Chorltonville, Opening of a New Garden Suburb.
3 Mr Alderman Gibson, Competition by Manchester Department, Manchester Guardian, January 26, 1911
4 Lawrence Beedle, 2017

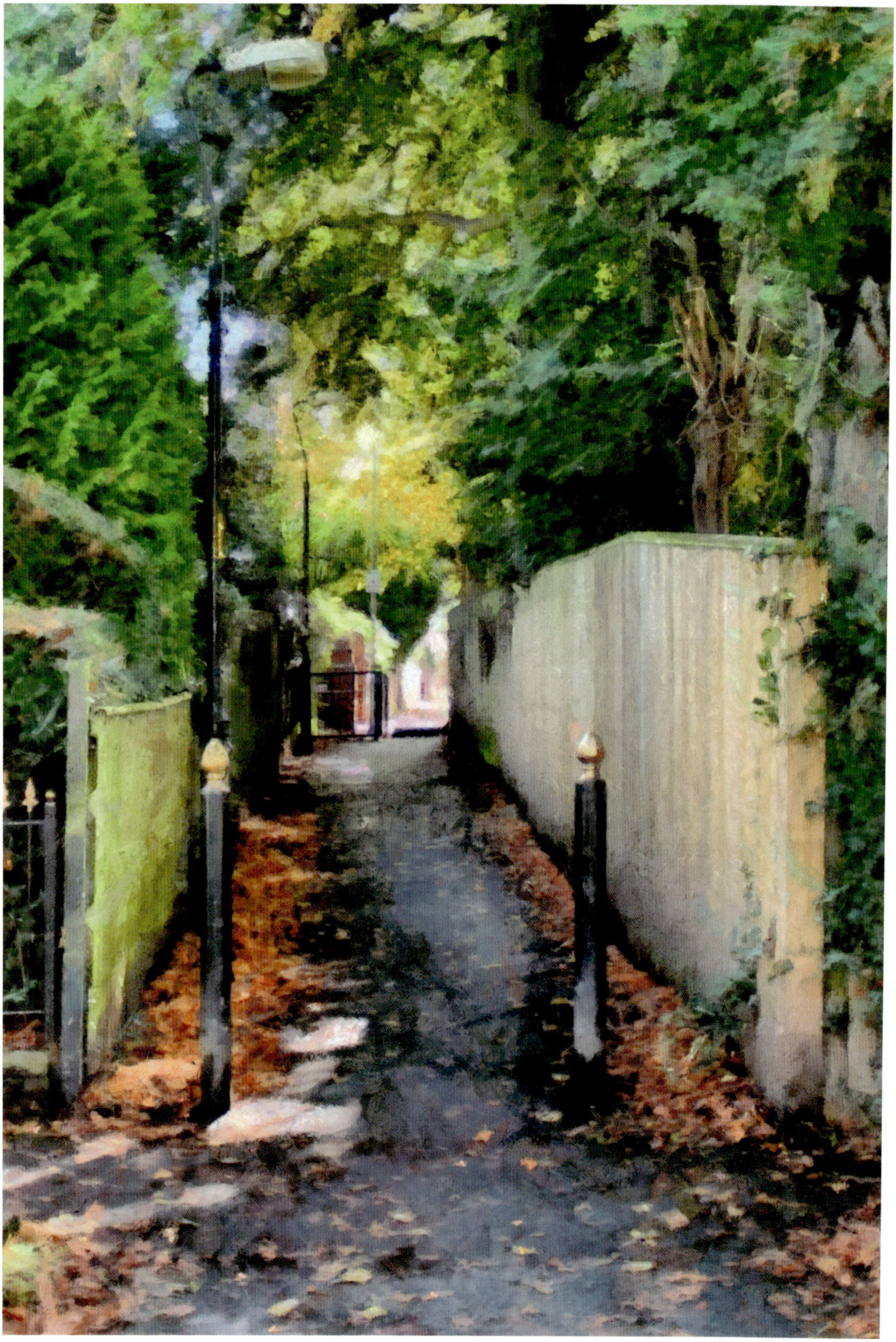

Holland Wood and The Cliffs circa 1900

The Stumps and other things...
a little bit of an ancient footpath on the edge of Chorltonville.

I doubt if many people give a second thought to the Stumps which lead from South Drive to Hurstville Road.

It is one of those convenient routes out of the estate, which by degree leads up to Hardy Lane and Barlow Moor Road.

And it is part of an ancient footpath which led from Hardy Lane to what is now Brookburn Road, which in turn offered a route past the old parish Church, and off west and south to Turn Moss, and eventually Stretford.

The romantic in me will sometimes walk that path; armed with an old OS map, I travel the fields, which had names like Smith's Field, Holt and Calf Croft.

And just before we would have reached the village, the footpath offered up unobstructed views north to the Brook, and a strip of wooded land known as the Cliffs.

But enough of this romantic tosh. By 1912, the walk would have taken me past the new houses of the Ville with their neat gardens, and maturing hedges and trees. By now, the estate had become a community, with its own bowling green, tennis courts and "Children's Corner".

The sports pavilion date unknown

And the "Ville", regularly featured in the newspapers of the 1920s and 30s, which reported extensively on the success or other of its Lawn Tennis Club, which was a private members club, and held an open tourney against other local clubs every June from 1923 to 1936.

Occasionally, the media was less than generous, and more than once took a side swipe at the residents.

In 1932 the Manchester Guardian in a review of the opera Die Fledermaus at the Opera House, described the audience as a collection of middle class worthies who obviously lived in Chorltonville or Pinner, wearers of plus-fours at the weekends, or at suburban bridge parties".[1]

All a bit unfair, but perhaps flags up that simple observation that the estate has been seen by many as a bit up itself, and a target, which certainly was the case just seven years later, when Dusty the Con Man made his appearance.

According to the Manchester Guardian, "dustmen were anxious to identify a quiet spoken and neatly dressed man, who, on the day before the annual round of the houses in Chorltonville for Christmas boxes, made his own tour, with highly satisfactory results. He had a little-notebook and a pencil, and insisted upon the householders entering their own

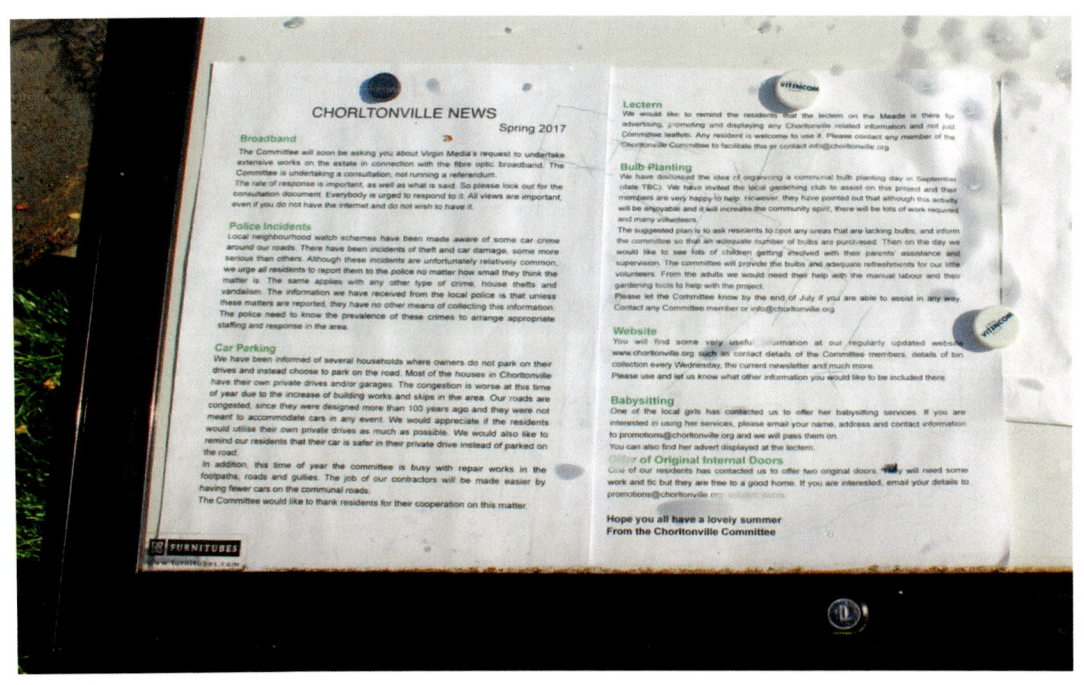

Chorltonville News 2017

names, together with the amount of their contributions. One of the victims said he was impressed by his insistence, and also his polite manner. On completing his round, he had three pages filled with names and contributions, ranging from one shilling to half a crown, and his haul must have run into several pounds".[2]

A century and a bit on, the Ville continues to be a community with its own newsletter, and strict rules about the upkeep of the estate.

The average asking price for a property in the "Ville is £600,000, which is a far cry from 1933, when the estate agents of R. C. Stonex & Sons, St Mary's Gate offered a "splendid house occupying a corner position in Chorltonville; 2 rent, 4 beds, garage, gardens; chief rent £5.10s; bargain at £725".[3]

The original Chorltonville housing company was wound up in 1922, having recorded profits over the years since it began.

At the dissolution of the company, it was suggested by the chair that a special fee of £1,400 should be paid to the seven directors, but the shareholders were having none of it, and by

1 The Opera House, Manchester Guardian, March 9, 1932
2 Dust in their eyes, Manchester Guardian, January 31939
3 Classified Ad 55, Manchester Guardian November 9 1935

a large majority they voted down the plan, and after "further discussion it was agreed the total amount should be £750".[1]

Such is the "power of the people". As for the grand plan of a rented estate, the houses were sold off, in some cases to existing tenants, and through the next two decades the properties were often sold in batches.

But we will close with a delightful description from 1926, which was part of a long article reflecting on the merits of the city.

"Chorltonville is one of the few parts of the city which may fairly be said to be self-conscious. Like a fortress on a promontory, it lies flung out from the old village green of Chorlton proper, and it is as remote from its natural ambitions as the fortress would have been to the hamlet which once perhaps stood there.

Chorltonville is something of a garden city. It lives up to its ideals by a multiplication of gables and grass plots. Most inclinations of roof may be seen in Chorltonville, except the Chinese, and in its own way is as romantic as the German

The Meade 1975

turrets.... Its roads too are named for effect. They sound like cottage industries, arts and crafts, raffia work and lattice windows".[2]

South Drive 1930

1 Chorltonville Directors, Manchester Guardian, February 1, 1922
2 Chorltonville, Literary Associations, The Manchester Guardian, October 2, 1926

East from the "Ville" and on till morning or Darley Avenue, whichever comes first...[1]

a trip that will take the reader from the edge of Chorltonville, via Cundiff Road and Hardy Lane, and on into West Didsbury.

Now, I am well aware that anyone with either Geography O level or a CSE will instantly pick up on the fact that Darley Avenue is in West Didsbury, and not in Chorlton.

But for the purposes of the book and this story, we will just have to bend the boundaries.

And back in 1929 the Manchester Guardian also chose to ignore such a demarcation, and published two pictures looking out from the same back window of a house in South Drive, with the caption, "these two photographs taken from a house in Chorltonville, illustrate the rapid growth of the new Manchester estate in Barlow Moor Road. That on the left was taken last September, and shows cornfields with Hardy Lane in the distance. In the other picture, the fields are covered with unfinished buildings of the estate".[2]

Those houses will be some of the properties on what is now Cundiff Road, which leads in one direction to Hardy Lane, from where it is a short walk to Darley Avenue, and thence a

Hardy Lane with Chorltonville in the distance date unknown

slightly longer stroll to Barlow Moor Road and Southern Cemetery.

The significance of the cemetery will become clear later, but for now, dear reader, it is the Cundiff Road and Darley Avenue estates which will fill the pages.

They were what we now call social housing projects and were desperately needed, as the Corporation made clear during its bid to acquire land around Barlow Hall Farm and Darley Avenue in September 1929.

There were, it pointed out, 10,000 names on the housing waiting list, added to which there were also 20,000 houses in the city which were overcrowded, and it made sense to build on what was farmland, given that south Manchester was, "where the population was spreading and was the only district which offered considerable opportunities for development".[3]

Already, the Corporation was planning to build 1,500 homes in Chorlton-cum-Hardy, for which they had received 3,191 applications.

1 "second star to the right, and straight on till morning" Peter to Wendy, Peter Pan, J.M.Barrie, stage play, 1904, novel, 1911
2 The Growth of a City, The Manchester Guardian, June 6, 1929
3 Land For Houses, Manchester Guardian, September 4, 1929

There had been three objections to the West Didsbury scheme. One came from the Manchester and District House Builders' Association, which argued that the land was suitable for a "larger type of house than the Corporation proposed to build", and that no development should take place till the estate at Chorlton-cum-Hardy had been completed.

It was an objection which some may think had a lot to do with the potential loss of the site for private development.

That said, the second objection which came from Mr Wright of Barlow Hall Farm, seems more heartfelt. He had taken the farm over just eight years earlier and "sunk a considerable sum of money into his holding on the assumption that he would not be disturbed for many years".

His plight seems all the worse for having already had his farm in the Rusholme district taken from him, for a similar housing scheme.

Alas, Mr Wright was not successful and the estate was built, which in turn led to the development of shops along

Barlow Moor Housing estate 1930

Hardy Lane Co-op Barlow Moor Road 1959

Barlow Moor Road and Mauldeth Road West, and ultimately the last of our cinemas, which was built beside Chorlton Brook on Barlow Moor Road, and had a variety of names in its history.

Of the new shops, the one that stands out and deserves special attention, is the Co-op Store on the corner of Hardy Lane and Barlow Road.

It was opened in 1929 as a co-operative shop, and still trades as one today; moreover, it is the only one left in the city which retains its hall, which is used by various community groups from the Labour Party and Co-operative Party to the Woodcraft Folk.

It was originally two shops, consisting of a butchers and grocers with stables at the rear. The meeting room upstairs could hold 100 and, for half a century, displayed on one wall was the banner of the Manchester and Salford Co-op Mixed Guild. It had been founded in 1931, at "an exceptionally well attended meeting of members who had the privilege of listening to many fine addresses given by our visitors,[1] representatives from the board of management, the educational committee, and the district committee of the National Guild of Co-operators".

Mottram Avenue from Barlow Moor Road 1952

1 Manchester & Salford Co-operative Herald 1931 page 211

And recently it had a makeover, but in the move to make all things modern a few of the old items from the upstairs hall have been retained, including the wooden tea trolley, which has done sterling service for half a century or more bringing the Co-op tea and Co-op biscuits to a thirsty audience.

At which point is worth mentioning just how many products and services the Co-op were engaged in selling. In the great days of co-operation it was possible to feed the family, and clothe them, choose just the right furniture to fit in the room beside the co-op wireless, and plan for both a holiday with aunt Edna, while being mindful that grandmother might soon need the service of the funeral department.

It was a shop for everyone from cradle to grave and no doubt was visited on occasion by Mrs Fullaway of Aycliffe Avenue,
 it is only fitting that we should continue on to Aycliffe Avenue, which is reached by turning off Darley Avenue on to Maitland Avenue, proceeding on to Mersey Bank Avenue and taking the first turning on your left into Aycliffe Avenue.

And such a convoluted journey is rewarded with the house that George Best stayed in as a young member of Manchester United. There was apparently a Club policy that young single members of the team were required to live in "digs", which in this case was the home of Mrs Fullaway in Aycliffe Avenue.

Now, I have to admit that it must be decades since I encountered the word "digs", which comes from a time long before now, when young single people far from home rented a room in a family home in return for which they got a bed, three meals a day, and maybe even had their laundry done for them. The upside was, you didn't need to worry about iffy canteen food, had someone who might be a friendly face, and

George and Mrs Fullaway, Aycliffe Road date unknown

you may even have been invited into watch the family TV. The downside, of course, was that you were in someone else's house, and pretty much lived by their rules.

It is usually associated with students, but both mum and dad spoke of living in digs when they first came to London, and my uncles always referred to digs while moving from one job to another.

I never found the idea attractive and instead chose bedsits in which to live, when I first came to Manchester.

But digs and bedsits have, I suspect, had their day, although they will still exist in slightly different and, I suspect, more up market versions.

All of which is indeed a long way from Chorltonville, Cundiff Road and even Darley Avenue, so, with that in mind, it is on further east from Darley to Barlow Moor Road and Southern Cemetery.

SOUTHERN CEMETERY
A magical place of wildlife, fascinating history and powerful memories.

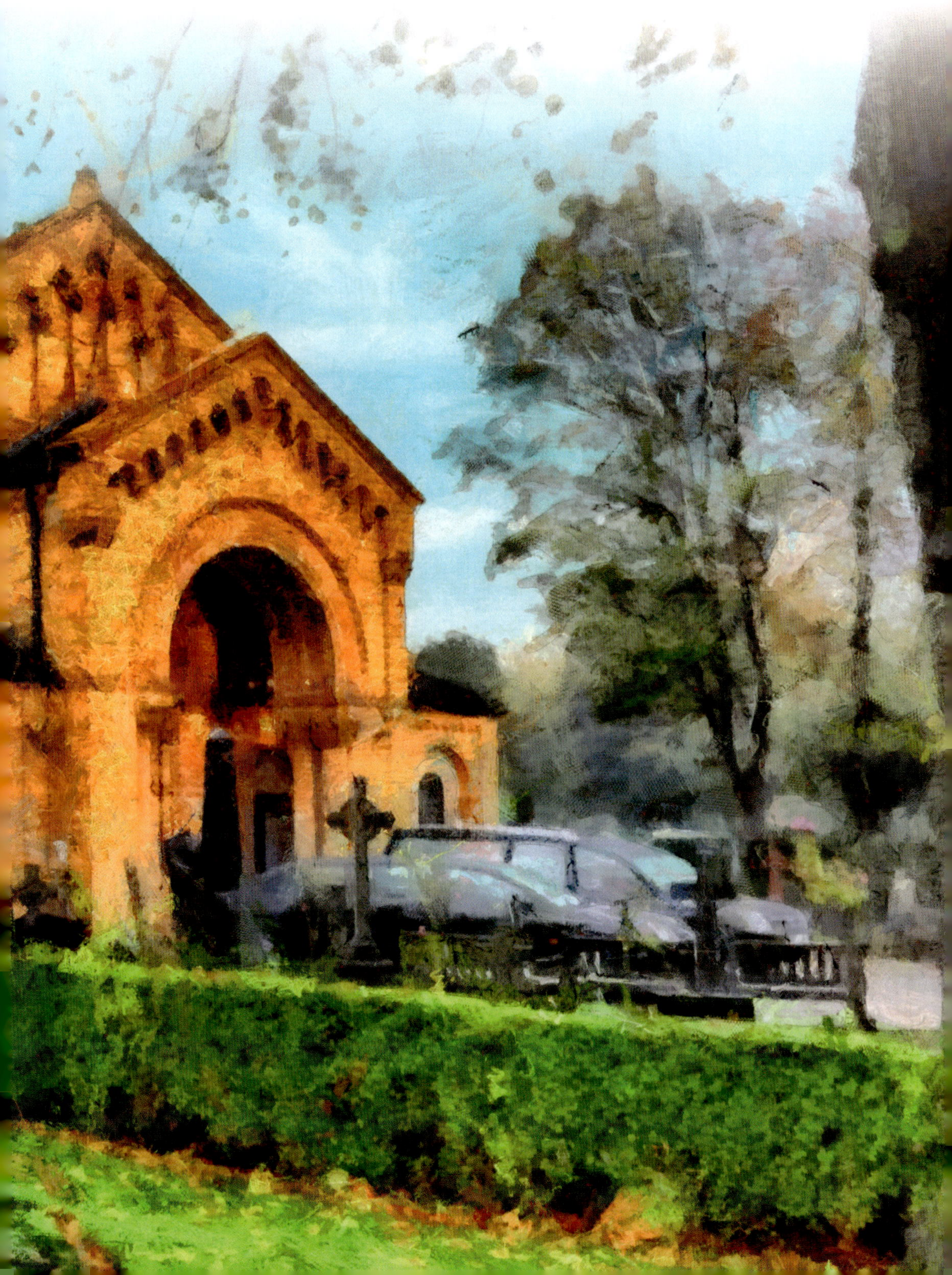

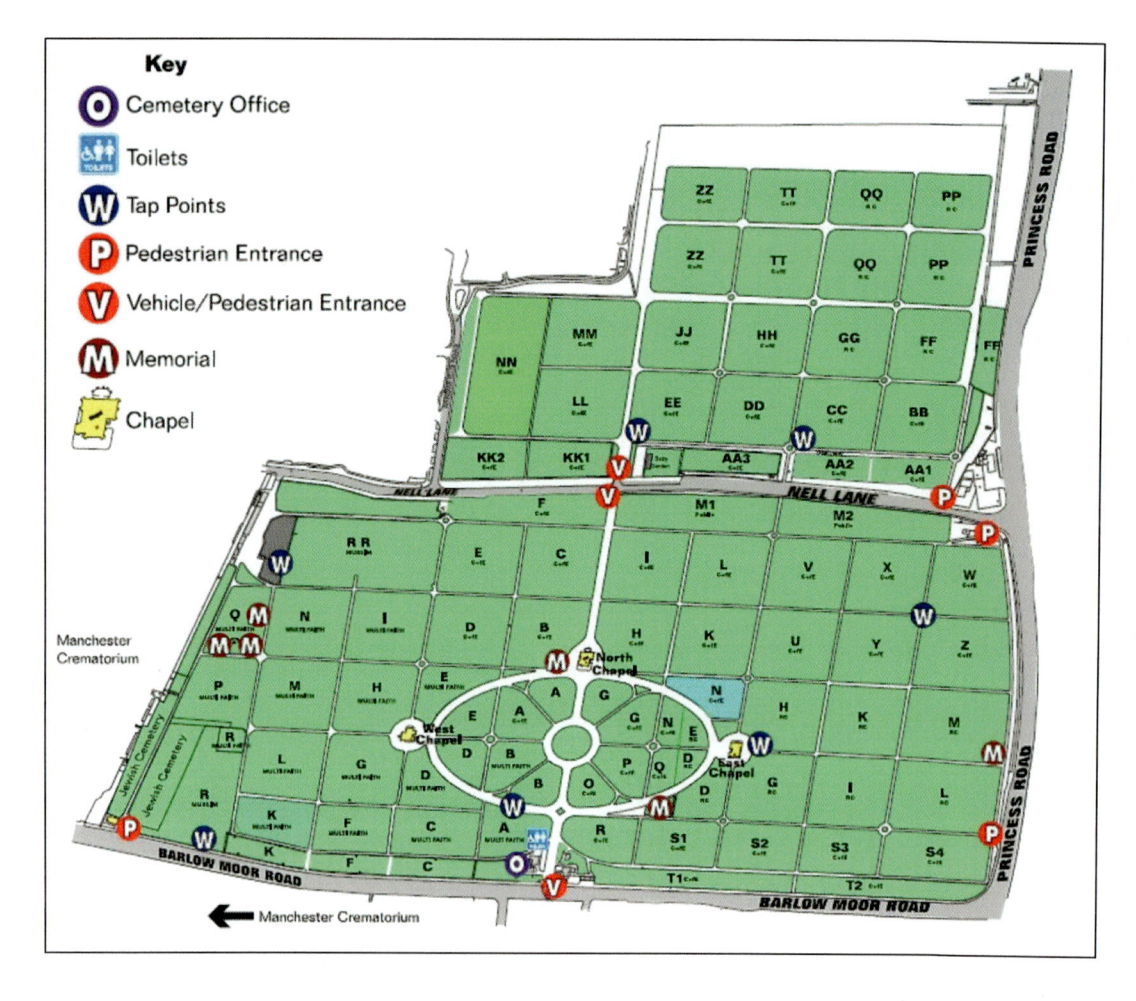

Southern Cemetery is that vast expanse of land running east from Barlow Moor Road to Nell Lane and, while its main function is that of a cemetery, it offers much more.

It teams with wildlife, is a regular venue for both heritage and nature tours, and contains a unique exhibition of memorabilia from both the world wars.

On any one day, it hosts a mix of people, from those visiting a gravestone to those just wanting to sit in a quiet place amongst the trees, or, better still, stroll along the wide avenues, taking in the changing seasons.

There are, as you would expect, a number of entrances both from Barlow Moor Road and Nell Lane into Southern Cemetery.

But of these, the grandest has to be through the huge iron gates, which afford one of the best views of the cemetery.

80

To your left are the offices, while to the right there is the Remembrance Lodge, of which more later.

The broad road leads onto the circle path, with the North Chapel ahead and the West and East Chapels on either side.

And here can be found some of the most impressive gravestones, which shouldn't of course detract from all the other memorials to those who are buried here.

Many are plain stone or marble headstones with little embellishment other than a name, a date and a simple inscription, but then there are those burial sculptures which draw you in, like the one near the entrance with a woman sitting atop a rock with an open book, or the tall figure of an Armenian woman.

Many of course are symbolic, and play to a set of ideas about how to portray grief, like the broken pillar which symbolises a life cut short, and the frequent use of angels.

Southern Cemetery 1925

A new cemetery for the south of the city, fit for purpose...

"The Public Parks and Cemetery Committee with reference to a new cemetery for the southern portion of the city... is to advertise freely in the newspapers for an advantageous site".[1]

So commented Alderman Murray in the September of 1871, but despite his purposeful report, even he had to qualify the plan, with the observation that there had been no reply to adverts and in consequence, "the Committee were in communication with owners of land on the south west side of Manchester".

And, as we know, those conversations proved successful, which is good for our story and was even better for all those relatives who wanted a new and suitable cemetery in which to place their deceased loved ones.

In 1872, the Corporation bought the 100 acre site for £38,340, and the following year awarded the contract to Mr H. J. Paull of London and Manchester.

But "owing to the difficulties connected with obtaining an outfall for the necessary drainage of the land, the works were postponed for nearly three years", and only began after the successful construction of a sewer to the river Mersey, which was two miles away.[2]

And for those who revel in fascinating facts, before work started, the "water stood throughout the ground at about three feet below the surface and permeated the substratum of sand down to the clay, about 15 feet deep. This had to be tapped, and the water drawn off, before the foundations for the buildings could be put in, consequently, the contract for the chapels and lodges was not let until May 1877".[3]

At which point the curious passersby would still not have seen much to excite them for another year, because the workmen had to dig down to the clay levels and then build concrete piers and brick arches for the foundations to rest on.

All of which might make the reader ponder on the sagacity of the landowner who sold off the 100 acres, especially as a cursory glance at maps from the 1840s and 50s show a fair

Southern Cemetery 1889

1 Alderman Murray, Manchester City Council, Manchester Guardian September 7, 1871
2 The New Manchester Cemetery, the Manchester Guardian, May 23, 1879
3 Ibid, The New Manchester Cemetery

number of ponds and culverted water courses, but far be it from me to quarrel with the wisdom of the Corporation's land surveyors.

And for those wanting more on the civil engineering work, I will just say that the water was drained away down "Barlow Moor Lane and Hardy Lane to Jackson's Boat where it discharged into the Mersey".

Despite all these watery obstacles the cemetery was opened on October 9 1879, and just in case anyone was still unsure of where the place was, one newspaper gave very clear directions commenting that, "the distance from the city boundary to the Cemetery via Chorlton Road is 2¾ miles, and via Withington 3½ miles. From the White Lion Hotel, at Withington it is a mile and a half, and from the Horse and Jockey Hotel, Chorlton-cum-Hardy it is only one mile".[1]

The Corporation had retained what they considered, "the most valuable of the trees that were found upon the estate", and added plenty of younger ones along with lots of shrubs.

Sadly, not all the chapels which were built are now open for use, which is a shame given that the Manchester Guardian was

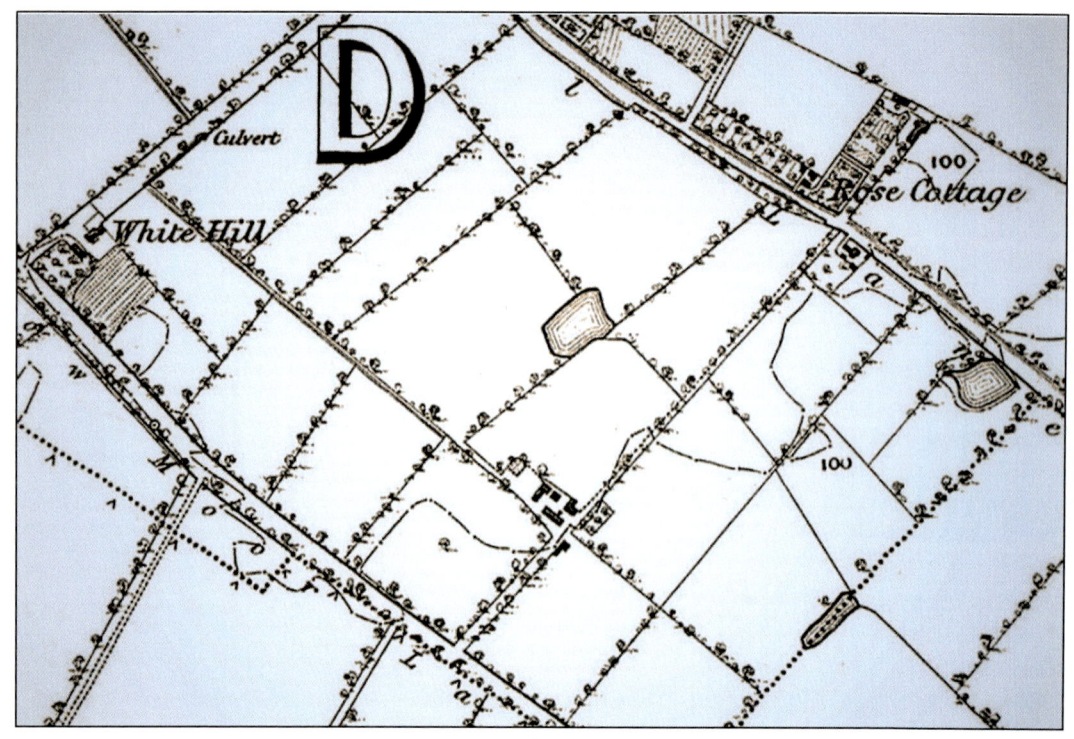

The land that will be Southern Cemetery 1854

of the opinion that along with the wrought-iron gates "they are very handsome".

I particularly like the idea that in the turret above the porch of the lodge was a bell which was 2 metres in diameter, and was "intended to be rung for the guidance of workmen and clearance of the ground". It is still there but is no longer used.

Apparently, although the chapels also had towers which, at 85 feet, were a full 35 feet higher than the lodge turret, they were not given a bell. But all three were impressive enough, with each having capacity for 80 mourners, and were fitted out with mortuary chambers "for the reception of coffins during the time of the service, [which were], separated from the chapels by glazed screens".

But each of the three also had "a decidedly varied appearance from the other", which I suppose underlined the difference in doctrine.

I won't be alone in having visited all of the three 1879 chapels, but today only one of the three remains open. The remaining buildings include the Jewish Ohel, which is the room

1 The Manchester Southern Cemetery, the Manchester Guardian, September 12, 1879

From David Harrop's permanent exhibition

used for prayers before the burial takes place, and the Crematorium which was opened in 1892.

The Manchester Cremation Society had been founded in 1888 and it set up the Manchester Cremation Company in 1890, with a capital of £10,000 raised by subscription.

It bought a plot of 6.75 acres of land close to Southern Cemetery, upon which it built a Crematorium with a chapel and a covered walkway with niches for urns. It was officially opened on October 2nd 1892, and was only the second crematorium to be opened in the country.

But the number of cremations remained low, so that in the first ten years there were only 471, which may have had something to do with the cost.

"The price of a basic cremation was £5-5s-0d, and to this could be added a further £1-1s-0d for the clergyman and 15s-0d for burial of the ashes in the grounds.

A niche would cost a further £2-12s-6d in the outside columbarium, or £5-5s-0d inside the chapel, to which a further £1-1s-0d would be added for carving the inscription on the slab.

By comparison, a simple burial for an adult might cost as little as 10s, or for a child 7s, with the clergyman charging a further 2s 6d. Furthermore, a

From David Harrop's permanent exhibition

86

burial plot might be available close to home, while cremation would involve a time consuming and costly journey to the one crematorium in south Manchester".[1]

Sadly, some of the registers and most other early records of the Crematorium were lost when the company's office in York Street was destroyed during the December Blitz of 1940. But the list of the first 412 cremations up to 1900 is available in the library at Clayton House, and, while those from 1900 to December 1940 have been lost, it may be possible to find a reference in a local newspaper death notice, or a memorial plaque at the crematorium.[2]

The most recent of the buildings at the Cemetery is the Remembrance Lodge which dates from 2008, and is for the use of families and friends wishing to pay their respects and remember loved ones.

The Remembrance Lodge also houses a unique collection of memorabilia from both world wars, as well as the history of the Postal Service.

[1] A Brief History of Cremation: The Manchester Experience, originally published in the Manchester Genealogist Volume 37/2 in 2001, http://www.mlfhs.org.uk/articles/37-2_cremation_history.pdf
[2] Ibid, A Brief History of Cremation:

Memorial, Piccadilly Gardens, 2016

The collection belongs to David Harrop, and it includes letters and official documents as well as medals, photographs and a collection of porcelain figures. Many of the items on display have a direct link to Manchester, and in particular to men and women associated with Southern Cemetery.

Some of those people are commemorated on the large collective war memorials, like that dedicated to the men, women and children who perished during the Manchester Blitz, along with those British and Commonwealth servicemen who died in both world wars.

Along with these, there are those memorials dedicated to the Tenerife Air Disaster of 1980, and the Katyn Massacre of Polish officers in 1940.

But above all, the cemetery is as it was intended, a place to remember the lives of individual people and in some cases whole families.

Memorial to the Manchester Blitz, Piccadilly Gardens, Southern Cemetery 2016

Sir John Alcock 1919

Amongst these, there are the great and the good, from war heroes, to industrialists, to musicians, and artists, a sprinkling of celebrities and even a philosopher and a mathematician.

The group is a long one, but some so fascinated our Peter, that he felt moved to put down the paint brush and wax lyrically about his memorable ones.

Like Sir John Alcock who, together with Sir Arthur Brown, made the first non-stop Atlantic flight in 1919. There is a blue plaque on the wall at number 6 Oswald Road commemorating his life. He is buried in Plot G 966.

Sir Matt Busby lived on Kings Road and was Manager of Manchester United for the best part of 25 years. Plot G 997

Matt Busby with European Cup 1968

89

Sir John Rylands, entrepreneur, philanthropist and multimillionaire, he gave his money away to lots of good causes, and is famous for the John Rylands library which can be seen in the centre of Manchester. Plot E 201.

Wilfred Pickles, comedian and star of stage, screen and radio. One of his famous catch phrases was "Are yer courting?". He died on 27th March 1978 and is buried in Plot I 1012.

John Rylands 1888

Wilfred Pickles Turf Cigarette card 1950

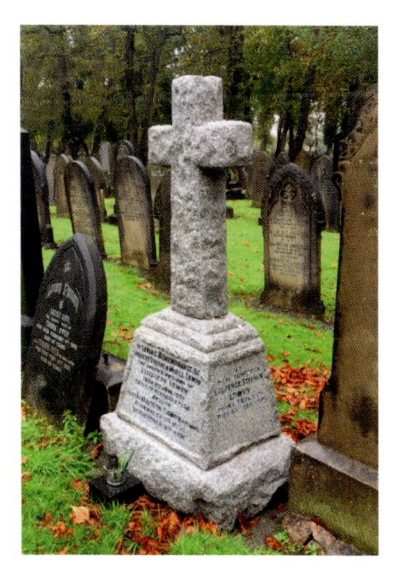

L. S. Lowry at New Cross 1968

L. S. Lowry, best known for his matchstick men and industrial landscape paintings, was a famous Manchester artist, born in Stretford on November 1st 1887. His father died in 1932 leaving a great deal of debt, which drove his mother into depression. She took to her bed until she died in 1939. Lowry became a rent collector which provided a stable income and much of his later life was spent looking after his sickly mother. It wasn't until the last 25 years of his life that he became famous. He is buried in the same Plot as his parents, C 772.

The others are all listed in the footnotes, allowing those with an interest to visit a particular grave and make their own discoveries.[1]

Finding someone buried or cremated in the cemetery is relatively easy. There is an online data base for both burials and cremations, which can be used in conjunction with a plan of the cemetery.[2]

For most of us however the importance of Southern Cemetery is that it offers a place of tranquillity where, if you want, you can contemplate an individual grave stone and ponder on the stories behind the names, or just sit and take in the beauty of the place.

1 Daniel Adamson, Samuel Alexander, Thomas Barker, Philip Baybutt, Henry Brougham Farnie, Rob Gretton, Howard Hawker, Henry Kelly, Ernest Marples, Billy Meredith, John Prettyjohnn, Cyril Ridley, Mark Schofield, Henry Gustav Simon, Anthony Wilson Grave or cemetery burials, Municipal and private cemeteries,
2 www.manchester.gov.uk/info/324/family_history_searches/7374/grave_or_cemetery_burials

View across the cemetery 2010

The Armenian grave 2010

And for those who want to learn more, there are those guided tours. Emma Fox runs regular heritage walks around the cemetery and Tony O'Mahony gives occasional nature walks looking in particular at the wild life.[1]

There is also the Friends of Southern Cemetery, which is a community group.

All of which just leaves me to reflect on that other attraction of almost all big cemeteries which, along with expanses of grass, trees and neglected internments, are the conkers. Yes, conkers, because when you are nine, the beauty of the memorials and the tranquillity of the place are nothing compared to the huge numbers of freshly fallen conkers.

But to get them you have to enter the place without being seen, which usually involved climbing over the high railings in the early evening, so as not to come across any one. But that in turn meant you ran the risk of forgetting the time, and being caught as dusk fell, which is not so good an idea.

I remember one day late in September, when my friend Jimmy maintained there was always a huge pile to be had amongst the gravestones of the departed. All went well until it became apparent that we had been caught out by the time, and with the light fading fast it did not seem such an inviting place. Moreover, it was difficult to retrace our steps towards the safety of the outside, and so, bit by bit, the tall trees and the imposing gravestones took on a more sinister and menacing appearance.

Graves 2014

Funeral symbolism 2014

1 Emma Fox, tel 07500774200, email showmemanchester@yahoo.co.uk, facebook & twitter @showmemcr

93

BARLOW MOOR ROAD
And on to Manchester Road.

NatWest

Barlow Moor Road and on to Manchester Road

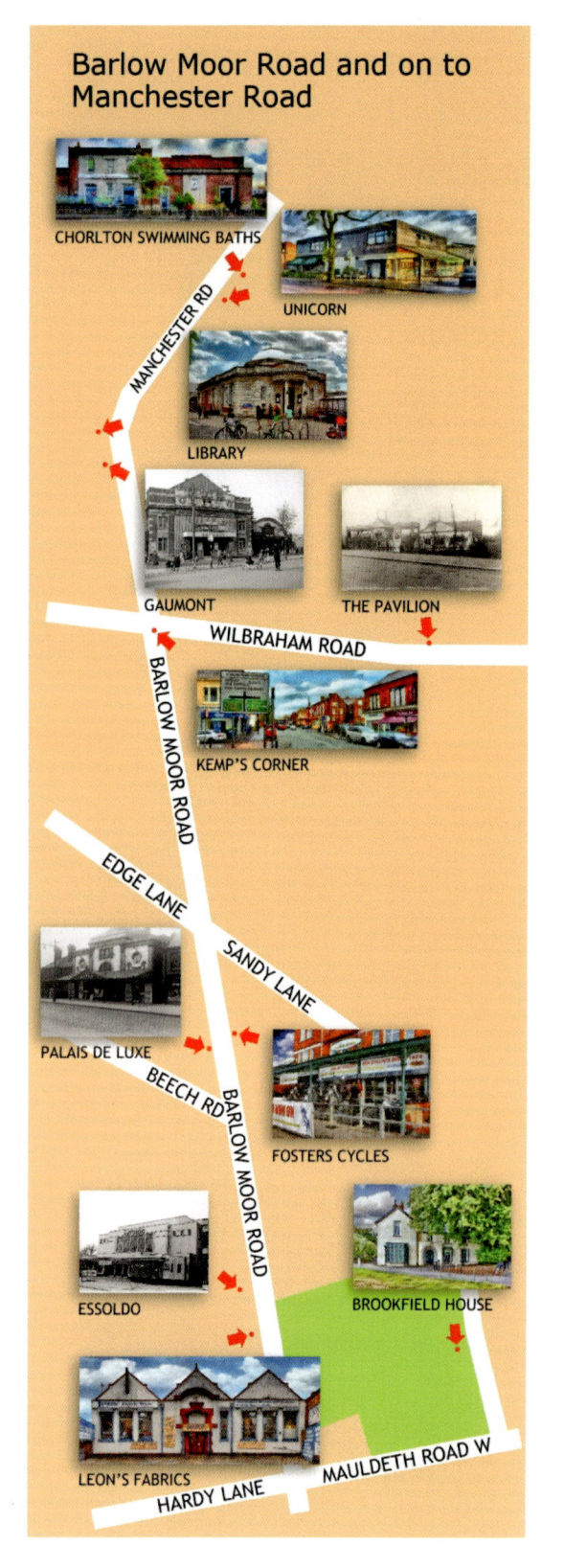

[Map with locations marked: CHORLTON SWIMMING BATHS, MANCHESTER RD, UNICORN, LIBRARY, GAUMONT, THE PAVILION, WILBRAHAM ROAD, KEMP'S CORNER, BARLOW MOOR ROAD, EDGE LANE, SANDY LANE, PALAIS DE LUXE, BEECH RD, FOSTERS CYCLES, ESSOLDO, BROOKFIELD HOUSE, LEON'S FABRICS, HARDY LANE, MAULDETH ROAD W]

Once known as a lane but not even worthy enough to get into the history books.

Now while it may well offend the Friends of Barlow Moor Road, this great strip of highway running from Didsbury through Chorlton and on to Manchester Road, gets little of a mention in the annals of Chorlton-cum-Hardy.

Mr Booker, who wrote his history of Chorlton in the 1850s, ignores it, and thirty years later, our own Thomas Ellwood can't find it in himself to write about it.

And that is a bit unfair, given that he describes the old road that led out of the village to Stretford, the new toll road built by Samuel Brooks from West End to Brooks Bar, and the road, "at the eastern end of the village via Sandy-lane, passing Sandy Brow, Moss Cottages and Dog House Farm, thence through the townships of Moss Side and Hulme to City-road, and Chester Road".[1]

But the coming of the Corporation tramway in the early 20th century put Barlow Moor Road properly on the map and led to a widening of the road and, of course, our new tram terminus by Beech Road.

By then, it had been elevated from a lane to a road, a new bridge over the Brook had been constructed, and the old farms which had stood beside it had vanished and in their place we had a park, two cinemas, lots of new shops and much more.

And had you walked a bit further, you would have passed the new road cut by Lord Egerton in the 1860s, tarried at Kemp's Corner, and strolled on past our Temperance Snooker Hall to a third cinema and the municipal Library and Swimming Baths.

All of which will appear in due course in the story.

Barlow Moor Road 1925

1 Ellwood, Thomas, Roads, Chapter V1, the History of Chorlton-cum-Hardy, The South Manchester Gazette, December 12 1885

Chorlton Park, and more than a few surprises...

"Chorlton is at present poorly endowed with public places, the only existing space being Beech Road Recreation Ground".[1]

So wrote the Manchester Guardian in the April of 1925. It was an observation that the people of the area could have said was startlingly obvious, and had been so since the building boom of the late 19th century covered the township in rows of terraced and semi detached houses.

As early as 1892, one local resident had complained that, "Chorlton will soon be as crowded as Alexandra Park, but without the park", and suggested using a small plot of open land between Wilbraham Road and what are now Corkland and Zetland Roads, as a public open space.[2]

It says much for the period that the writer

Brookfield House Chorlton Park date unknown

expected the land and the maintenance of the park would be achieved by public subscription.

In the event, it never happened and the plot was built on, leaving us without a large public place until 1928, when, in the May of that year, the Corporation opened Chorlton Park.

Plans had been set in motion three years earlier, and the park was to have "twenty hard tennis courts, four grass tennis courts, two bowling greens, a children's paddling pool, an open-air swimming bath, and a number of pitches for cricket and football". The grass tennis courts were to be reserved in the afternoon, "for children who will be charged 1d per hour".[3]

The once fine Brookfield House, which may date from the late 18th century, and in its time was home to a doctor and boasted a large pond, became the home of the head gardener and remains a fascinating building, although sadly, nothing of its original interior features have survived.

Aerial view Chorlton Park 1933

1 The New Chorlton Park, Manchester Guardian, April 9 1925
2 Manchester Guardian May 24 1892
3 A New Park for Manchester, Manchester Guardian, March 31, 1928

A goat and a bag of food circa 1960s

And in the way of these things, that swimming pool has also vanished. It was 50 yards long, 21 yards wide, and it ran from 5 feet 3 inches at the deep end, to 2 feet and 6 inches at the shallow end.

There are plenty of people who remember it, along with the small animal reserve, which at one time had goats, rabbits and much more. All are now just a distant memory, as is the sunken bandstand, which was surrounded by semi circular terraces, which protected the audiences from the wind.

Looking at the one image we have, it was less a conventional bandstand and more an open air theatre.

It was located a short distance from Brookfield House, and included a stage behind which was a stone clad building. The stage was protected by a flat roof which was supported by brick columns, and the whole thing was finished off with more columns, adorned by ornamental features.

It was impressive enough, but I suspect did little to placate the residents in the houses by the Beechwood Avenue entrance

Corporation Destruction Works Nell Lane 1925

to the park, who muttered darkly and loudly about how the ground was being levelled by, "tipping the ashbin contents of the district to form final levels".[1]

The Parks Department was swift in denying the accusation, responding that the material used at the Brookfield Avenue entrance, "consisted of either good tipping material, or of refuse which had passed through the incinerator. No dustbin refuse was used, which had not been treated by the destructor", although it did concede that some raw ashbin refuse was used near Nell Lane, "but this was immediately covered up".

Now, I have no way of knowing, and would not want to impugn the integrity of the Park's Department official, but there will be plenty of people on those allotments beside the entrance who have turned up more than their fair share of clay pipe fragments.

Fragment of clay pipe Beech Road 2014

1 Chorlton's New Lung, Park Department Reply to Criticism, Manchester Guardian, March 1 1927

101

There are too many to be accounted for by careless farm workers, and while it is just possible that they are the result of earlier deposits of night soil, brought from the city in the middle of the 19th century to spread on the land, I rather think the Parks Department was not entirely truthful.

All of which just leaves me to ponder on the hidden water course that flows through the park, and which had disappeared into its brick culvert long before Prince Albert welcomed his Queen to the opening of the Great Exhibition in 1851.

But for those wanting a link with that distant past, it is still possible to walk through the park, and follow the route from Barlow Moor Lane up to the entrance of Hough End Hall, and

Brookfield House and surrounding fields 1854

imagine catching a first sight of that fine Elizabethan hall, in the company of old Sir Nicholas, who built Hough End in 1596.

And a little under three centuries later, a lodge was built at the Barlow Moor Road end, on the north side of the lane, and called Hough End Lodge.

But it, and a portion of our route vanished with the building of Mauldeth Road West which, in 1925, the city council planned would replace the ancient lane with a "new 100 foot road branching from Princess Road and running across the fields to Hardy Lane [which] will be also be widened", leading to the disappearance of Jackson's footbridge, "to be taken by a fine county bridge giving a new outlet from Manchester to Cheshire".[1]

It is of course one of the quirks of history that things didn't quite turn out as planned for, while Mauldeth Road West was built and Hardy Lane widened, a proposed tram route had to wait a century, and the "county bridge" never did replace the old foot bridge.

1 Bringing Blackpool to Hulme, the Manchester Guardian, June 16, 1925

Leon's, the date and the mystery...
the fabric business which was once a printing press, and started as Mrs Keal's dream.

Now there is something very odd about the date on the wall of 419 Barlow Moor Road.

Most people will know the place as Leon's the fabric shop, but I have long wondered why the building carries the date 1885, when it was built around 1915.

The Leon family began trading there in the 1990s, and before that it had been the Addressall Print Works, which is listed in the directories by 1921 and, for an even shorter time between 1915-17, it was the Chorlton Laundry owned by Mrs Keal.

Not that this helps with the date of 1885, which appears above the door, along with the word Established.

Now, it is just possible that the date refers to either the establishment of the laundry or the printing company, but there is no reference to Addressall in any of the directories in the late 19th century and anyway, the stone lettering looks like it was done when the building went up.

So I rather think we must be with Mrs Keal, who was running a laundry business on Beech Road in 1894.

That said, there is no evidence that she was trading before that date, and in 1881 Mr and Mrs Keal were living in Croydon, but by 1889, they had settled in Chorlton, and were running a business from No. 30 Wilbraham Road.

Mr Keal described himself variously as a brick layer or builder, and I suppose it is just possible that the date 1885 refers to the start up of his business.

Either way in 1915, Mrs Keal was in that building on Barlow Moor Road operating the Chorlton Laundry.

Now, I can't be exactly sure when she moved in, but in the April of that year, Mr Keal of "Brookbank Bridge Barlow Moor-road died at Chorlton Laundry Brookbank Bridge".

And just over a year later the business went bankrupt.[1]

According to Mrs Keal, at the bankruptcy hearing in the February of 1917, "the main cause of her coming into court was the shortness of loose working capital, when she removed to her new premises on Barlow Moor Road, after having carried on a similar business on less extensive lines for many years in Beech Road, Chorlton".

To advance Mrs Keal's dream of running the new laundry, she had spent over £900 on new machinery, in the expectation that she would retain the contract from the military hospitals in Manchester.

But the military authorities had established their own laundries, just as she was finding it difficult to obtain sufficient labour which, she told the hearing, "had made it impossible to get the work done as promptly as the hospitals required". It was a state of affairs compounded "by her inability to pay higher wages" to attract more labour.[2]

And, despite addressing the "weak point in her business affairs", she was forced to close, moving to St Annes-on-Sea, where she died in 1935, leaving £2625.

Addressall Printing Works 1959

1 First Meetings and Public Examinations, The London Gaztette, February 16, 1917
2 Laundry Proprieters Ill-luck. Failed with a surplus of over £3000, Manchester Evening News March 6 1917

The cinemas, just 80 and a bit years of flickering magic...

from the performing Whips and an Ice Rink, to the one with a posh name, the one that now deals in funerals, and the one Mr Hitler bombed.

The cinema came early to Chorlton-cum-Hardy, and in the 80 or so years that Tom Mix, Humphrey Bogart and Sophie Loren marched across the screen, we saw five picture houses come and go and, while not all of them were situated along Barlow Moor Road, two were, while a third was on Manchester Road. The remaining two were on Wilbraham Road and Longford Road, and these two should not form part of this story but, as Emerson said, "consistency is the hobgoblin of little minds".

Strictly speaking, he actually wrote, "foolish consistency is the hobgoblin of little minds", but I have no intention of clouding a good link with an accurate quotation. Suffice to say that it makes perfect sense to group all five together, even though Peter will tell me off because it will make nonsense of his fine maps.

Now, for any one born in the first half of the last century, the word "Flicks" will be one that was interchangeable with "the Cinema", "the Pictures", or "the Movies" and perfectly described that magic of flickering pictures, which moved across the screen.

And there was also something intriguing about the names of individual picture houses which reflected this new and exciting form of entertainment, ranging from the Kinemacolor Palace to those incorporating the word "electric", of which my favourite was the Bijou Electric Theatre, or the exotic sounding Trocadero, and Alhambra Pavilion.

Most also incorporated the title "Picturedrome", and some went through frequent name changes.

But what they all had in common was that magic of sitting in the dark, and seeing moving pictures many times life size, telling stories of adventure and romance set in faraway places, which for most people, were just names on a map.

Our earliest was The Pavilion on Wilbraham Road, which stood on a thin strip of land between the railway line and Buckingham Road. It was known variously as The Pavilion, or the Chorlton Pavilion, and later added The Winter Gardens to its title. It could hold an audience of 800, and had been

The Pavilion and Winter Gardens, circa 1910

109

operating as a variety hall from the early 20th century.

But it didn't entirely turn itself over to moving pictures. In June 1910, it offered a mixed variety bill, including The Whips, who were a singing and dancing troupe, and four years later hosted the Chorlton Operatic Society's performance of "Dorothy", which was a comic opera, with a plot based on mistaken identities, and a series of absurd comic situations.

Inside the Palais de Luxe 2010

Memories of The Pavilion have yet to disappear, and my old friend Ann remembers her father talking of visiting the cinema to watch the cowboy star, Tom Mix.

For a short time, the Pavilion was challenged by the Longford Picturedrome, on the corner of Longford and Oswald Road.

It first came to my attention when I came across a painting by J. Montgomery, who painted the place in 1946, from a photograph dated 1906

He referred to it as "Chorlton Skating Rink (later the Picturedrome)", and there is a reference to it as the Chorlton Skating Rink when it was wound up as a company in 1916.

Two years earlier it was listed as the Longford Picturedrome, seating 600, and its proprietor was a James Morland.

It had a short existence, and it may be that the competition with its close rival proved too much, or it was the Great War which finished it off.

Either way, I doubt that the cinema goers of Chorlton would have given

Detail of plaster moulding inside 2010

The Palais de Luxe 1924

it much of a chance, once the first of our grand cinemas was built.

This was the Palais de Luxe on Barlow Moor Road which opened in 1915, and is very similar to the old Grosvenor picture house opposite All Saints. Both were clad in green and cream tiles, and had the same elaborate designs around the windows.

Long ago, it exchanged films for the more basic stuff of groceries and soap powder, and traded under various supermarket names, from Hanbury's to the Co-op, and for a while was the service centre for Ready Radio, when it was photographed in 1962 with almost all of its old facade.

Sadly, that elaborate frontage is now hidden, but upstairs in what became the storage area, there are the remnants of the original plaster arch which stood above the cinema screen.

The Palais de Luxe as Radio Rental 1962

111

But there is one picture of the Palais de Luxe taken by local photographer Charles Ireland soon after it had opened, and the story behind that image is a little odd.

The original photograph is in the possession of the East Dunbartonshire archive, which is a long way from Chorlton and, at first, both the archivist and I were puzzled as to how it had made its way into their collection, but the clue was the glass and iron canopy which fronted the cinema. This had been made by the Lion Foundry just north of Glasgow, and its collection of documents and pictures are now held by the East Dunbartonshire Archive.

It is most likely that Charles Ireland had been commissioned by the foundry to take the picture of their ironwork. He ran the family photographic business on Lower Mosley Street, which he had taken over from his father. The family had lived first on St Clements Road, and later on the corner of Edge Lane and Kingshill Road, and in the early 1920s Charles and his wife Edith had moved into number 76 High Lane.

Advertising the week's entertainment at The Palais de Luxe 1924

Charles took the picture sometime at the end of April, or right at the beginning of May 1928. I can be fairly sure of the date because all the films listed outside were made between 1927 and 1928, and the billboard to the right of the entrance announced that, during the "week commencing May 7th" the cinema would be showing The Call of the Heart, Long Pants, the Climbers and Sky High Saunders.

It was a mixed bunch of films. The Call of the Heart was a Western featuring Dynamite the dog, Long Pants, a comedy with Harry Langdon, The Climbers, a historical melodrama located in the Spanish Empire during the reign of King Ferdinand VII, and Sky High Saunders was about a "daredevil pilot who took on all comers and prevailed, whether it was gangsters, good-or-bad women or bad weather".

Now to modern cinema goers, this seems a lot of pictures for just one picture house in just one week. But running times varied, so while Call of the Heart ran for 50 minutes the Harry Langdon movie was under half an hour.

It may be that the William J. Rees Orchestra, which was playing on the night the photo was taken, were there

Getting ready for the first performance, The Palais de Luxe 1924

accompanying the films, or perhaps giving a separate performance.

I have tracked Rees's career around the northwest during the inter war years, and this may have been one of his earlier orchestras.

Not that this is all the picture gives up. It was taken in the morning, the sign for the 2.30pm matinee has been placed by the entrance, and a cleaner is out front making the place ready.

Finally, there are the two buildings either side. Both have undergone many changes since 1928. To the left, the building was still in private use, but in the subsequent years became a doctor's surgery, cafe, antique shop and, more recently, a plumber's and a carpet outlet. To the right was the sweet shop, which in turn was next to Shaw's Motor Garage.

And because, "foolish consistency is the hobgoblin of little minds", I shall pay no heed to logical geography, and slip back along Barlow Moor Road to the Brookburn Bridge, where we would once have encountered Rivoli Cinema.

It was the last to have been built and was the last to close. It opened in 1936, and our own brass band played at the opening ceremony.

Allan Brown was there, and the icing on the cake was that he got in to see Errol Flynn in Captain Blood, which was one of Flynn's better swashbuckling movies.

Painting of The Rivoli 1965 from a 1940s photo

The box office was in the centre of the auditorium and, behind it, there was the sweep of stairs which took you up the circle.

Coming down from the stairs, you could look out through the great windows with their faded drapes to the Feathers opposite.

And, over the years, it managed a number of different names, becoming the Essoldo in 1955, the Classic in 1972 and finally the Shalimar, before closing in 1982.

From the Rivoli to the Essoldo 1959

CHORLTON

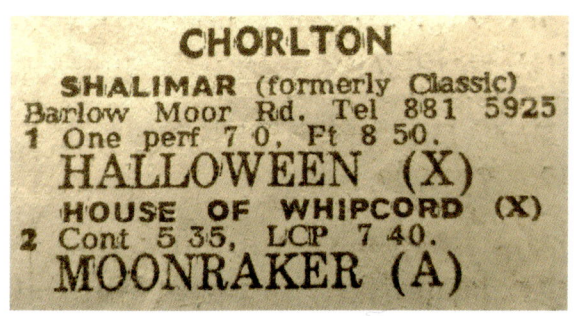

SHALIMAR (formerly Classic)
Barlow Moor Rd. Tel 881 5925
1 One perf 7 0, Ft 8 50.
HALLOWEEN (X)
HOUSE OF WHIPCORD (X)
2 Cont 5 35, LCP 7 40.
MOONRAKER (A)

Films to watch at the Shalimar 1980

As the Shalimar, it had the bizarre experience of being pictured on one cinema programme in 1981, with an entirely different looking exterior.

Nor is that quite all of the odd aspects of the Rivoli, for having been damaged in an air raid, it was used as a food store, only reopening in 1954, when, as part of the advertising campaign, the manager offered complimentary tickets for the restaurant.

Ida Bradshaw remembers her father receiving tickets and getting off work early to attend.

The restaurant continued to run through the rest of the '50s, and was popular as a lunch time venue, which has a sort of historic consistency, given that the site is now a fast food restaurant.

There will be some who maintain that the site of the cinema was the final home for Chorlton's branch of Blockbusters, but as appropriate as that would be it is not so. This building was once, according to Mr Stanley a "public market place", which closed

E Boydell & Co Ltd 1959

sometime before 1939, and then reopened as "E. Boydell and Co. Ltd, painting and finishing department, agricultural machinery".

The OS map for 1934 shows the site with a building which conforms to the present footprint, but with no name or explanation of its use.

It was still operating as E. Boydell and Co. Ltd in 1959, but a decade later had become a builder's merchants before its time as a cycle shop, the place to rent or buy Hollywood's best and not so best, and finally knocked down and rebuilt as a M&S Food Hall.

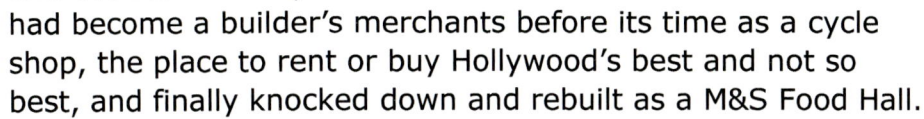

By which time our fifth cinema had gone the way of the rest. It closed in 1962 as the Gaumont, having offered feature films, news reels and Saturday Morning Pictures, along with choc ices, Kia-Ora and of course the Bee Gees.

And in the 42 years that it entertained the people of Chorlton, it changed its name from the Picture House, to the Savoy and finally ending up as the Gaumont, and at one time nearly became The New Majestic Cinema.

But most people will only know it as the Co-op Funeral Care.

Gaumont Cinema 1958

117

Foster's, cycles, a diary and a muriel...
one of the oldest businesses in Chorlton, and the one with a claim to an even older bit of our history.

Anyone who has followed Coronation Street since it was first launched in 1960 will remember Hilda Ogden, and that fine "muriel" of a mountain range, which Eddie the lodger and Stan her husband, pasted on the wall of their back room, to hide the fact that they run out of wall paper.

Hilda loved the scene and always referred to it as her "muriel", which I know Ken Foster would never do about his own mural painted by Peter, depicting the Four Banks, which rests on a wall in Ken's cycle shop.

It is a nice idea having your own bit of Chorlton's landscape for your customers to gaze at, as they stand in the shop pondering on

Sandy Lane 1925

118

Fosters Cycles 1959

119

which bike bell to buy.

They might also ask to see that other bit of our history which lurks behind the shop, and is all that is left of when the site was the dairy of Mr Fred Walker, who lived in Box Cottage, and Miss Mary Jones, who lived next door in Ivy Cottage and ran a laundry.

Now both cottages pre date the present row of shops, and stretch back well into the early 19th century. One of them will have been the shop of William Brundrett, who sold groceries from this spot in the 1840s and 50s, and gave his name to the junction of High Lane, Sandy Lane and Barlow Moor Road. Officially this was known as Lane End but like so many popular names it slipped into common usage as Brundrett's corner.

That floor from the days of the dairy

And Mr Brundrett's old house has been found, not once but several times. It turns up on several old OS maps and on the deeds held by Ken Foster, which detail the owners of his shop right back to 1912.

Deeds are a fabulous insight into the history of a property, for they not only list the previous owners but will tell you who owned the land when it passed from agricultural use to a building plot. In our case this was a Florence Ethel Holt Haig, who I have come across before. She was related to the last of the Manchester Holt's who owned land in Chorlton, including the stretch from Barlow Moor Road down to St Werburgh's.

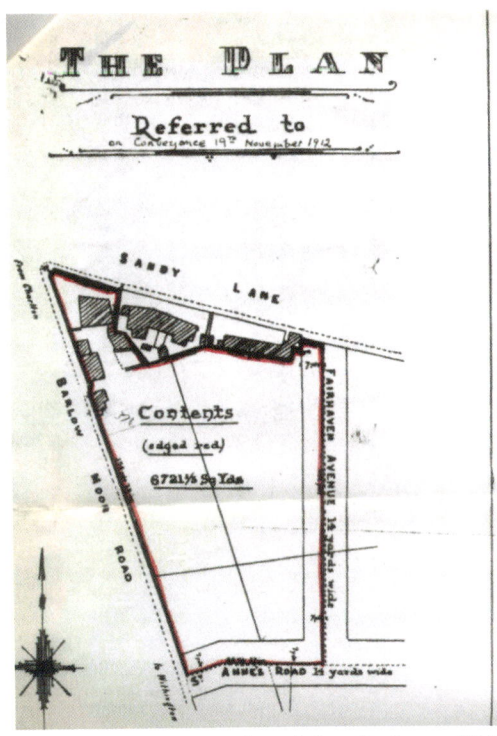

And with the death of Mr Holt the land was sold off, which in turn offers up a date from the

Barlow Moor Road and Sandy Lane 1911

deeds for the construction of the fine row of shops and houses of which Mr Foster's is located.

Equally fascinating are the two maps attached to the deeds, one showing the properties which existed on the site before 1912, including what had been Mr Brundrett's grocery store and the new buildings, measuring 6721⅓ square yards. That second map also reveals how the back yards bend to accommodate the geography of the plot.

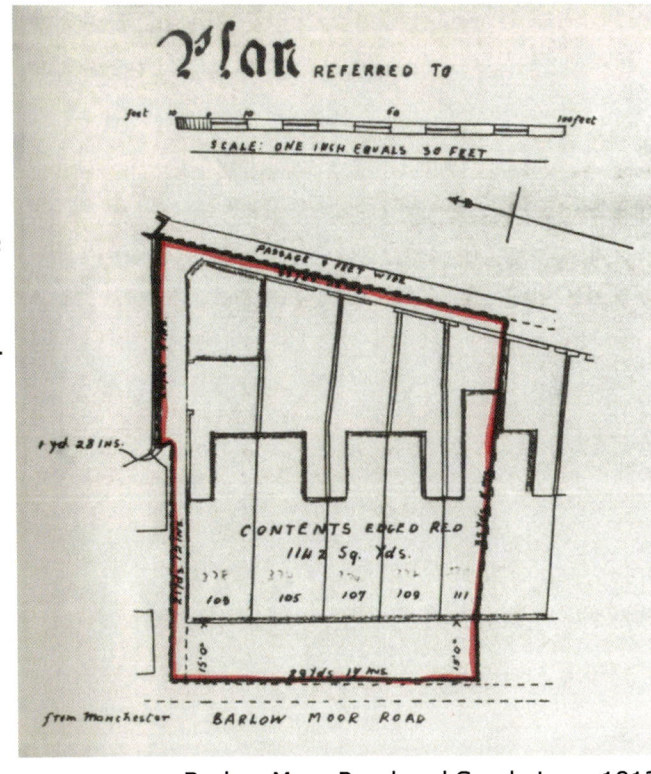

Barlow Moor Road and Sandy Lane 1912

121

Kemp's Corner...

Harry Kemp, chemist, one of our first City Councillors and a name that lived on long after his death.

I do like the idea that place names arise from common experience, and nowhere is this more the case than the junction of Barlow Moor and Wilbraham Roads. Officially it is Chorlton Cross, a name which seems to have slipped out of the Planning Department of the Corporation, sometime around the turn of this century.

But to most people it is the Four Banks, which makes perfect sense given that there is a bank on each corner, and much earlier it was Bank Corner, although back then there was only the one bank.

And that I suppose is why Bank Corner became Kemp's Corner, which was a more obvious title, because what today is the

The Clock at Kemp's Corner 1959

HSBC, was the chemist shop of Harry Kemp. It remained for almost a century the chosen place to arrange to meet for, not only was it in the centre of New Chorlton, it had a large clock above the door.

In an age before the mobile phone, and when fewer people had watches, Mr Kemp's premises made for a suitable landmark, which had the added attraction that you knew with a glance at the clock when your friend was late.

As such, it continued as a popular place to meet, and the name Kemp's Corner has yet to fade from living memory.

Mr Kemp had another chemist shop on Beech Road. and was one of the first three councillors elected in 1904 to represent Chorlton on the City Council. following the decision by a majority of rate payers to become part of Manchester.

Kemp's Corner circa 1914

The Library, "built in fulfilment of a promise made in 1904"...

Mr Carnegie's money, the plans that sank with the Titanic, and a 1904 electronic aid for learning.

Now, back in 1904, Manchester had promised the rate payers of Burnage, Chorlton, Withington and Didsbury an offer they couldn't refuse. In return for voting to join the City, the Corporation held out an offer of cheaper gas and water rates, and new, state of the art public libraries.

But the libraries were a little slow in coming. In the case of Chorlton, the first library was opened in 1908 in a rented house on Oswald Road, and it would be another six years before the purpose built one was opened on Manchester Road.

The new library was, "furnished with a thousand carefully selected volumes for use in the library and

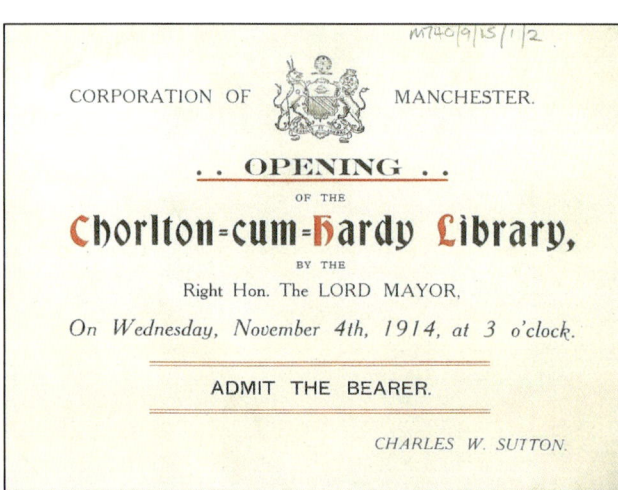

The Library is open 1914

124

home reading… a good selection of magazines is placed in a separate reading room [and] a special feature of the new library is the provision of a room for meetings of Home Reading Union circles and similar organisations".

The Manchester Guardian reported, "the style is Classical with Ionic columns in Portland stone and had 7,420 books, [which] if necessary can be increased to 10,500 volumes. There is a general reading room for adults and one for juveniles".

In an age which has seen libraries add computers to the resources available to the user, it is perhaps surprising that the Lord Mayor in opening the library over a 100 years ago, "hoped that someday there would be a kinematograph connected to our libraries for the special benefit of boys and girls, enabling them the better to understand the histories they were reading".[1]

It was an impressive addition to Chorlton, but one that had had more than a few hiccups, because the original plans drawn up and submitted to the Carnegie Foundation, which paid for the building, were lost when the Titanic went down.

Open for the use of all

1 A New Library, Manchester Guardian November 5th 1914

Nor did the idea of taking money from Mr Carnegie sit comfortably with everyone. He was an American steel magnate of Scottish descent, and our library was only one of 660 which he funded in Britain, 1,689 in the United States, 125 in Canada and more elsewhere, between 1883 and 1929.

From humble beginnings he had built up a huge steel business, before selling out for an estimated $500 million in 1901, and devoting himself to philanthropic projects. Even before he retired, he had been spending money on all sorts of projects, of which the establishment of public libraries was just one.

But there are those who would argue the money was not his to give away, having been made by the men who toiled in the steel plants, and who were increasingly denied the right to organise collectively in his work places. But that is another story.

Here in Chorlton, the charge against the Carnegie gift was led by Councillor Jane Redford, who, "was not infatuated with the Carnegie gift" expressing "a feeling of disappointment that the Chorlton ratepayers were not to get a library through the ordinary means of municipal enterprise".[1]

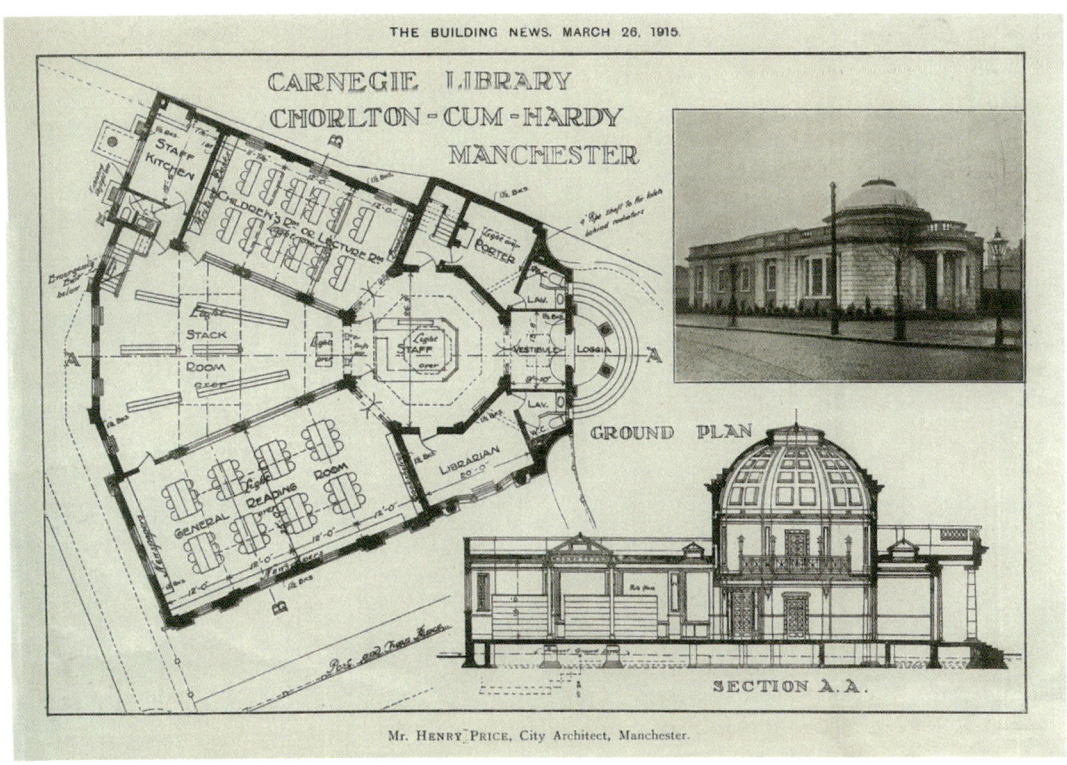

Inside the Library 1915

The Library 1914

1 New Library for Chorlton, Manchester Guardian September 28 1911

127

Unicorn, a Chorlton co-operative since 1996 with a roof garden and pond...

offering a huge range of affordable, wholesome food with a focus on organic, fair-trade and local sourcing.[1]

The idea of co-operation as a business model is an old one and plenty of us will claim we can remember our "divi number". I will be honest and say I long ago forgot ours and, as a child, was relieved when the Royal Arsenal Co-operative Society switched to issuing stamps.

Before Unicorn 1958

That said, we were at the heart of the Co-Op ideal. We lived on an estate built for Royal Arsenal workers in 1915 and purchased by R.A.C.S whose headquarters were just down the road in Woolwich, and I worked in their food warehouse down by the River Thames in the 1970s.

We even have a few of those thin metal tokens knocking around, which were given out by our local milkman.

But enough of such personal stuff. Instead, I shall return to Chorlton and the Co-operative ideal, and point out that there were several Co-op shops in Chorlton, including one on Barlow Moor Road hard by the Royal Oak, another on Beech Road and the store up by Hardy Lane.

And, while the traditional Co-operative stores found business increasingly difficult, during the closing decades of the last century the idea of co-operatively owned enterprises was alive and flourishing, from Credit Unions, to retail operations and building schemes.

Which neatly brings us to Unicorn, whose history can be accessed on their site. Suffice to say, they began in 1996, and have grown over the years developing the site they now occupy.[2] But I will say because this is the bit I like, they added solar panels in 2005, and a rooftop pond and wildlife garden in 2007, and most recently, a large kitchen, where they make fresh 'ready to go' food for the shop.

1 Unicorn, Who we are, http://www.unicorn-grocery.co.uk/who.php
2 Manchester, the Manchester Guardian, September 20, 1929

Chorlton Swimming Baths, a second promise fulfilled...

"it has two swimming baths – one for men and one for women, wash-baths and a suite of Turkish Baths".[1]

The baths are the end of the journey, and it is fitting that we should finish where we began with another promise made in 1904, but only fulfilled years later. Along with the promise to build the library, the Corporation had also offered to provide swimming baths. And if the library was overdue by a decade, the swimming baths took even longer. In 1915 there had been moves to buy land beside the railway for the sum of £730, and five years later the City Council was seeking to raise money to acquire the site.[2]

Finally, in the September of 1929, we got those baths, and perhaps the wait was worth it. According to the Manchester Guardian, a large crowd gathered outside on Manchester Road and, while the building, "could not be described as a thing of beauty, it has two swimming baths – one for men and one for women, wash-baths and a suite of Turkish Baths".[3]

The cost to attend the Turkish Baths was half a crown, which The Manchester Guardian reported would allow, "the people of Chorlton to lie for half an hour or so in a pale blue

Inside the swimming baths 1929

1 Manchester, the Manchester Guardian, September 20, 1929
2 Manchester Pubs The Stories Behind the Doors, Chorlton-cum-Hardy, 2017, Topping Peter, & Simpson Andrew, pages 106-107
3 Ibid, the Manchester Guardian, September 20, 1929

room amidst blue sofas and blue curtains" concluding that "thus has luxury come to Chorlton".

That said, Miss Annie Lee, speaking on behalf of the City Council at the opening of the Baths, argued, "that it was time we ceased to think of the Turkish bath as a luxury invented for the sole use of elderly and obese millionaires".

Now that is a sentiment I approve of, and I would like to have met her. She was born in 1875, and was elected to represent Gorton South as a councillor in 1919, and was the first woman Alderman on the City Council.

Inside the swimming baths 1929

As a member of the Labour Party on the Council, she successfully opposed the Education Committee's attempts in 1922 to reintroduce the pre-war regulation which prevented married women from becoming teachers. The prohibition had been relaxed during the war, but authorities across the country began to reassert the ban, allowing only married woman, "whose husbands were unable to support them", or women, "who had great teaching abilities".

Miss Lee also campaigned in 1929 for the Public Health Committee to give instructions in birth control in Council clinics, was active on the old Board of Guardians, and later in 1930, on the Public Assistance Committee.

Alderman Wright Robinson recalled, she was "a woman who had the strongest convictions and stood by them fearlessly, whilst her independence could be described as

Doing the baths in style 1929

Outside the baths 1958

fierce. Nothing could shake her on such matters as Sabbath observance and opposition to Sunday games or equal pay for women".[1]

Many I think might be intrigued by that reference to, "Sabbath observance and opposition to Sunday games," but would concede that, in some instances, Sunday working has led to exploitation, and certainly the Gorton United Trades and Labour Committee were on record as expressing the opinion that, "the feminist and trade union causes owe her a great debt".

The baths are now closed and, while there has been some interest in reopening them as a private co-operative venture, there is also talk of a housing and retail development, which some have speculated could accommodate an overspill for the Unicorn.[2]

1 Alderman Annie Lee Obituary, Manchester Guardian October 26, 1945
2 Chorlton's Unicorn Grocery could be moving... to former Chorlton leisure centre, Beth Abbit, April 22, 2016, MEN, http://www.manchestereveningnews.co.uk/news/greater-manchester-news/chorltons-unicorn-grocery-could-moving-11223328

EDGE LANE AND WILBRAHAM ROAD
The ancient and the modern.

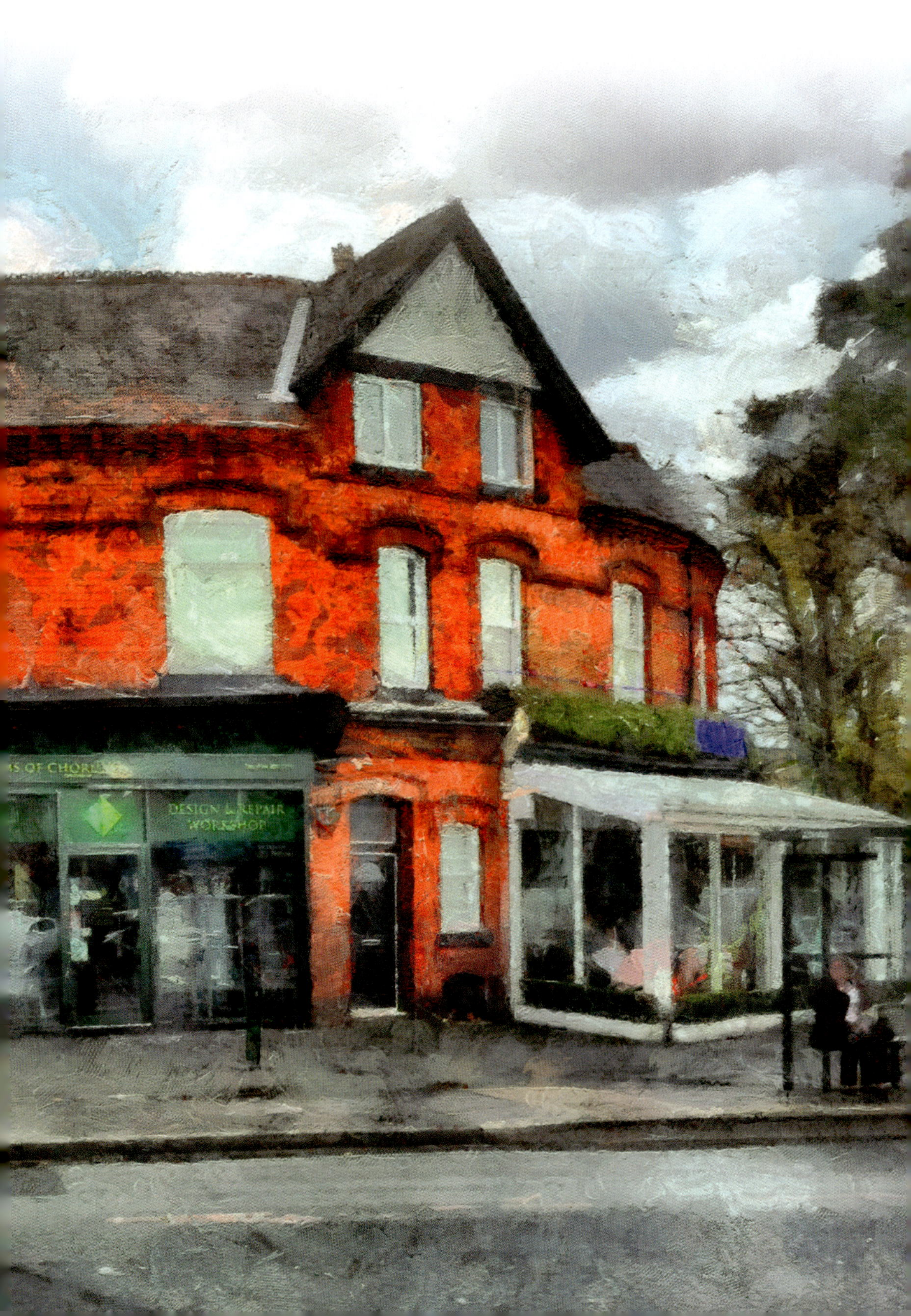
DESIGN & REPAIR
WORKSHOP

Edge Lane and Wilbraham Road

LONGFORD PARK

CHESTER RD

EDGE LN

EDGE LN

BARLOW MOOR RD

REACH OUT TO THE COMMUNITY

HIGHFIELD

STRETFORD SHOPPING CENTRE

WESTONBY

WILBRAHAM RD

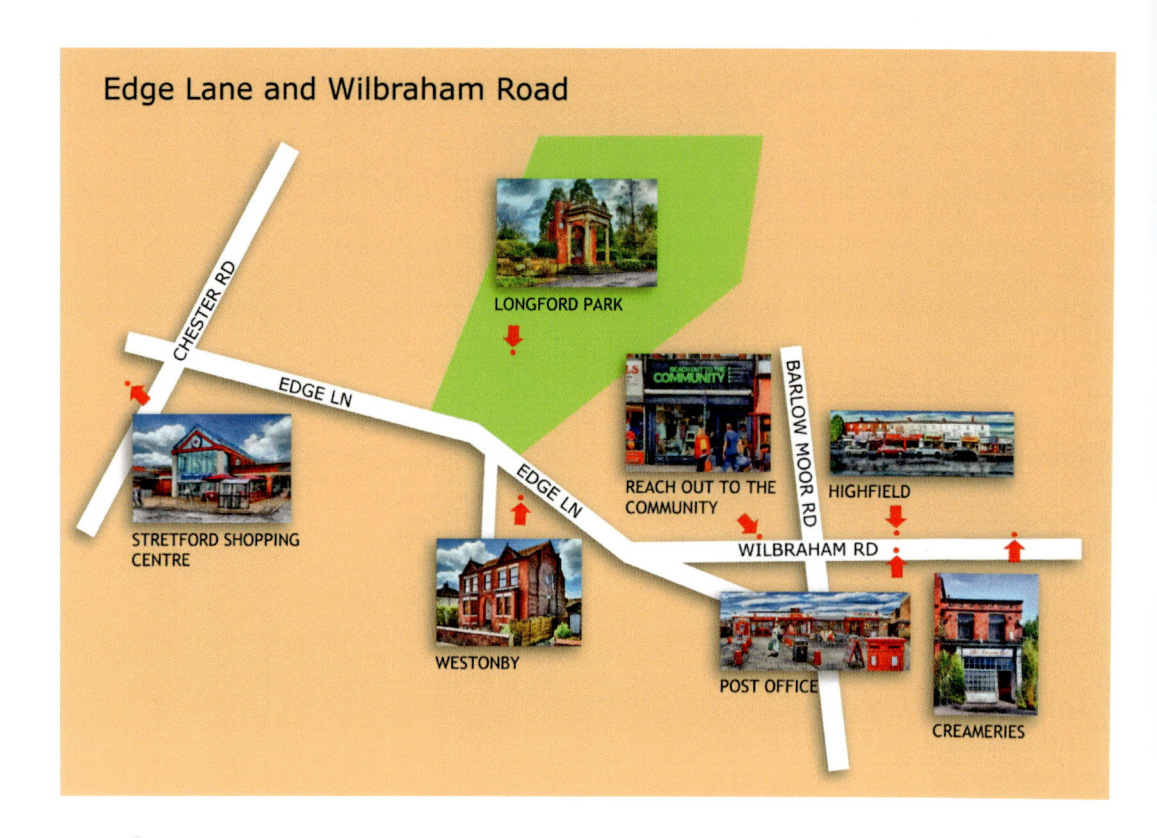

POST OFFICE

CREAMERIES

East from the Duke's Canal through Chorlton and on to Fallowfield.

Now, the Edge Lane and Wilbraham Road corridor takes you from the busy township of Stretford across a chunk of south Manchester, before ending up at the other great highway that travels north from Didsbury into the city.

Edge Lane is very old, but not so Wilbraham Road, which was cut in the 1860s, and runs pretty straight all the way to Fallowfield. Back in the 1850s, the Egerton's considered three routes, all of which crossed close to Red Gate Farm, which is the site of the library.[1]

Our own historian Thomas Ellwood, writing in 1885, confined himself to the observation that, "it was formed some sixteen years ago by the late Lord Egerton, father of the present earl. It extends from Wilmslow-road at Fallowfield to Edge-lane, along which a main sewer runs to within a short distance of the railway bridge at Chorlton station.[2]

From here it passes through the fields to Barlow Moor-lane, adjoin Lane-end, crossing High-lane, Cross-road and Beech-road, thence through various gardens, finally emptying itself

The Egerton sewer meets Chorlton Brook possibly 1890s

1 Egerton Papers, M24 /1/15, Archives, Central Reference Library
2 Ellwood, Thomas, L, Roads and Footpaths, Chapter 6, History of Chorlton-cum-Hardy, South Manchester Gazette, December 12 1885

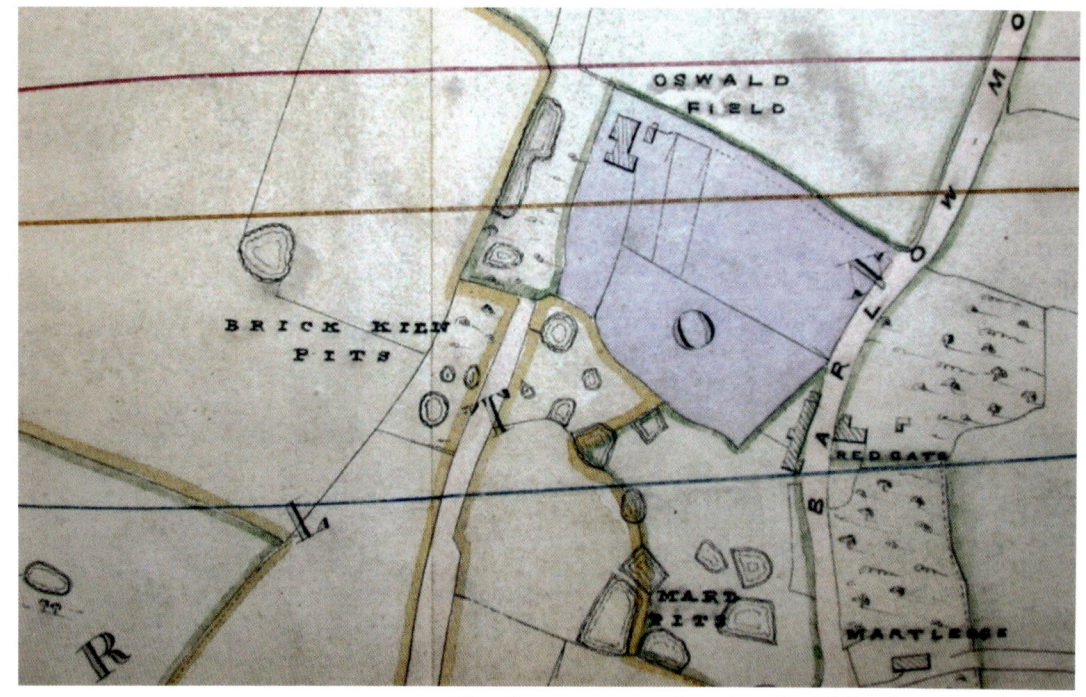

The three proposed routes for Wilbraham Road 1853

into the Chorlton Brook at a point about 200 yards below the bridge, which crosses the stream to Jackson's Boat".

So as far as Mr Ellwood was concerned, the road was less interesting than the sewer which ran beside it.

But for many it will be the reasons for the construction of the road and the benefits it might have brought to the township that are more fascinating. The map of the proposed routes is dated 1853, and shows all three ran north of the current line of the road.

The description with the map is less than helpful, confining itself to, "plan of projected new road from Rusholme to Stretford", and there are no accompanying notes.

The first marked in blue would have crossed Martlege, just below Red Gate Farm, the other two coloured brown and red would have crossed just a little further to the north, and two of these would have involved crossing Longford Brook.

Now why none of these routes was chosen is as yet unclear; there may have been issues with the land, especially around the Isles,[1] or it may have been because they ran close to Red Gate Farm and crossed Longford Brook.

All of which is one of those little bits of history yet to be uncovered, leaving me just to record that the final planned route incorporated a tiny section of Manchester Road, which I will leave for you to discover.

The decision to cut the road made perfect sense. The railway had come into Stretford in 1849 with its station on Edge Lane and, pretty much right away, within five years the first handsome villas were erected and these were steadily added to, until the housing boom of the 1880s made the Edge Lane Wilbraham road route almost a seamless line of properties, up through Chorlton as far as the railway station.

The rest of Wilbraham Road, from Chorlton to Fallowfield, would have to wait until the early decades of the 20th century, but in time these too would front Wilbraham Road, with a mix of fine Edwardian mansions, some smaller semi detached properties, and a council estate.

Another fine home, Merlewood House Wilbraham Road 1959

1 This is the area abound Longford Road which was popularly known as the Isles and was dominated by small lazy little water courses feed ponds and pits which had been dug to extract clay and marl

That place over the railway track, beyond the Dukes Canal, Stretford...

"the garden of Lancashire".

Now there is no logical reason to include Stretford in a book on Chorlton, but my friend Clive once lived there, and Peter still visits the shopping centre, added to which it does allow us to introduce the reader to two quirky Stretford nicknames.

Stretford, like Chorlton, was by the 1840s pouring its agricultural produce into the city. In 1845, over 500 tons of farm produce were going by road into the City each week from Stretford.[1] These carts were piled high with fruit and vegetables, of which rhubarb was a particularly profitable crop. The carts left Stretford just after midnight for the markets, and while one family member remained to sell the produce, the rest returned with the cart loaded with manure, ready to repeat the operation the following day.[2] This prompted one observer to describe the place as, *"the garden of Lancashire"*.[3]

It was also a major centre for the processing of pigs for the

Manchester market, as well the manufacture of black puddings, and had gained the nicknames of Swineopolis and Porkhampton. During the 1830s, between 800 and 1,000 pigs were slaughtered each week, and sent into the city.[4] Most came from Ireland, via Liverpool, and were transported into Stretford by barge. On arrival the pigs were kept in cotes, kept by the local landlords. The Trafford Arms charged one penny per pig a night, and had cotes for 400 pigs.[5] Not surprisingly in 1834, there were 31 pork butchers in Stretford, compared to one in Chorlton, and five in Urmston.[6]

Horse & Cart 1909

1 Scola, Roger, Feeding the Victorian City, Manchester University, Manchester, 1992, page 105
2 Leech, Sir Bosdin, Old Stretford, Privately Printed 1910
3 Ibid Scola, Roger, page 97
4 Cliff, Karen & Masterton, Vicki, Stretford: An Illustrated History The Breedon Publishing Company, Derby, 2002 Page 19-22
5 Brundrett, Charles, Brundrett Family Chronicle The Book Guild 1984 Pages 6-7
6 Pigot's Directory for Cheshire, Lancashire & Yorkshire 1834, page 538, Historical Directories edition page 338

Longford House, and our own Chorlton radical...[1]

"The great cause of liberty [which] *demands the steady support of the brave, the just, and the philanthropic".*

Now long before the Rylands built the impressive Longford Hall, there had been a slightly more modest Longford House in what is now the park, and it was for a while the home of our own distinguished radical politician, who ended up in court because of his support of the French Revolution.

This was Thomas Walker, one - time pillar of Manchester society, but also a radical politician who campaigned for the abolition of the slave trade, supported the French Revolution and was indicted for treason in 1794.

The family lived at Barlow Hall from the late 18th century, spending the summer there before moving back for the winter to their town house on South Parade, which faces what is now Parsonage Gardens. And it was there that a mob attacked Walker, who was forced to drive them off by discharging a pistol, in the December of 1792.

This was at the height of political debate over the issues of press freedom and the French Revolution.

"Emboldened by drink and fired on by agitators, groups hostile to the radicals began to gather around the city". Walker was in no doubt that this was pre planned. "Parties were collected in different public houses, and from thence paraded in the streets with a fiddler before them, and carrying a board on which was painted, with CHURCH and KING in large letters".

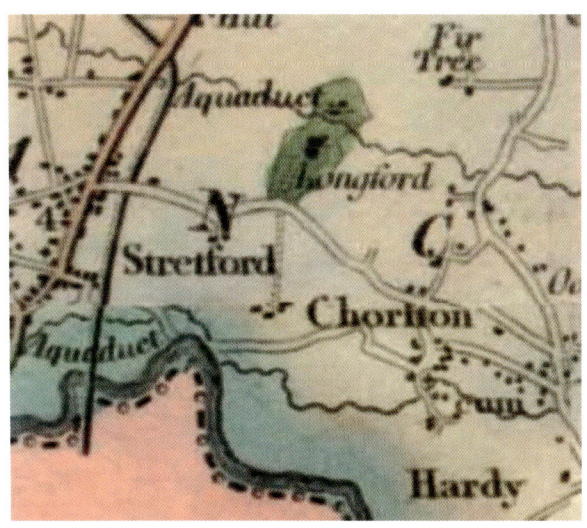

Chorlton-cum-Hardy 1830

On four separate occasions a mob gathered outside South Parade, broke the windows, and attempted to force their way in. Supported by friends, Thomas Walker was forced to fire into the air to disperse the crowds. The magistrates did nothing to prevent the events, and, while a "regiment of dragoons was in town, booted and under arms", and ready to disperse the rioters, no order was given. As if to add insult to injury, the main concern of the magistrates when they finally met Walker, was that he should not fire at the crowd again if the mob returned! These attacks had been matched by similar ones on the home of Priestly in Birmingham, and in Nottingham".[2]

Walker survived both the attacks and was acquitted of treason, after which he retired to the new family home at Longford House, where he died in February 1817, and was buried in the parish church on the Green.

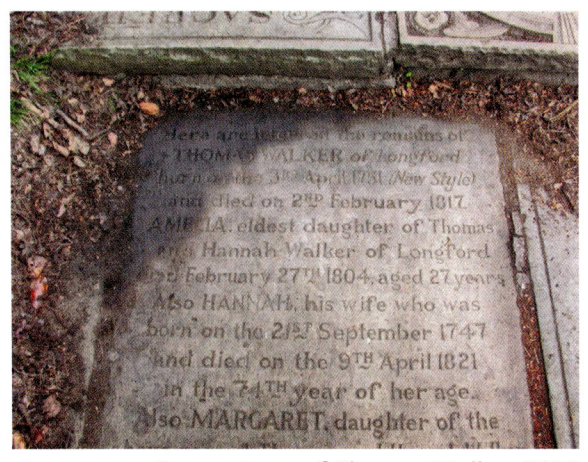

Grave stone of Thomas Walker 2008

1 Manchester Herald April 28th 1792
2 Walker, Thomas, Principles of the Church and King Club, Manchester, June 23 1792 page 19

143

Westonby and The Twilight Sleep Home for painless child birth...

the house just beyond Longford Park with a slightly odd story.

Westonby is a big Edwardian pile on the edge of Chorlton which was built in 1903, and was grand enough to have merited the following description: "cellared throughout, contains three well-lighted entertaining rooms; billiard-room spacious hall, five bedrooms, box room, bathroom, and separate W.C, lavatory and W.C on ground floor, excellent kitchen, usual conveniences and large garden... contains 3,074 square yards or thereabouts, and has a frontage of about 200 feet on Edge Lane".[1]

All of which made it an attractive place to live, but sometime around 1922 it had become the Old Trafford Twilight Sleep Home. Not I grant you the zippiest of names, and one with faintly comic overtones, and takes you back to one of those fashionable medical practices of the late 19th and early 20th centuries, and centred on the attempt to find a painless way for giving birth.

The standard approach had been to administer chloroform,

but in Germany experiments had been undertaken to see if women could give birth while asleep. The mother was given a mix of morphine and scopolamine ,and early results were so promising that by the early 20th century the method had been adopted in the USA and Canada.

Our own Twilight Sleep Home opened in 1917 on Henrietta Street in Old Trafford, and moved to Westonby sometime in 1921 or early 1922. It advertised itself as offering "Painless Childbirth" and featured regularly in the classified section of the Manchester Guardian until 1927. During those ten years its name varied slightly, but always retained Twilight Sleep.

The Westonby home does not feature after 1927, but its competitor on Upper Chorlton Road was still advertising in 1936, after which, it too vanished.

The answer might lie in the loss of faith in the medical practice. As early as 1915 there had been deaths associated with the method, and much mainstream medical opinion was at best lukewarm. There were also stories of poor quality care, and an absence of trained doctors and nurses, as well as horror stories of women having to be strapped to the birthing beds.

Despite its disappearance, The Twilight Sleep Home on Upper Chorlton Road continued well into the 1940s, and there are those in Chorlton who proudly told me that was where they were born.

Westonby Edge Lane 1914

1 Sales advert, Manchester Guardian, 1905

Reaching out to the community...
the only way we can make a real difference to the lives of people living on the streets, is by all working together to tackle the issues surrounding homelessness.

Now the history of the charity shop in Chorlton has yet to be written.

And before someone passes a sniffy comment about such a project, I would just remind them of how important such shops are, from the work they do and the people they help, to that simple observation that, without them, a lot of

Chorlton's retail units would be empty.

The trouble is, we tend to take them for granted, and I doubt many of us could say which charity opened up first, and how each of their stories has panned out, so that is the challenge should anyone care to take up the project.

Now Peter has made a start earlier this year, with a painting of Reach Out to the Community, which supports "people struggling with the most basic of needs: food and shelter".

It focuses on two groups: rough sleepers in and around the Chorlton area of Greater Manchester and local individuals and families who are in food poverty, especially those who are particularly vulnerable, for example the elderly".

He donated the painting to the charity, and for those who want to know more about the charity, just follow the link in the footnotes.[1]

At which point, I have to declare an interest because, in the course of clearing out forty years of clutter from our cellar, Steph and Becky took the lot. It involved two car journeys, 17 sturdy shopping bags full of books and CD's, a box of electronic

---

[1] Reach Out to the Community, Facebook: www.facebook.com/OutReachtotheCommunity
Twitter: https://twitter.com/ReachOut_Com

wizardry, and mum's collection of plastic roses, which came free with packets of soap powder in the early 1960s.

The roses had lain undisturbed, along with sets of picture postcards from several seaside resorts. Sadly, there were no risqué ones, but the collection remains a valuable history lesson in its own right. One of my favourites is of a windy Eastbourne, sometime in the 1950s, with the message on the back "Wish we weren't here".

This is one of the joys of charity shops, for along with the good they do, they are a cornucopia of past fashions and fads. In one corner you might turn up a genuine Lava lamp at a decent price, along with an LP by the Shadows, and a clutch of old 1950s knitting patterns.

Our Jill, who roams the charity shop chains, has a mission not only to save these knitting patterns, but press them back into use. Her portfolio stretches back into the 1930s, and stops just forty years later, with a fine pattern from 1971, which has

Knitting patterns 1950s

a special place for me, because the original was used to knit me a jumper with a zip and collar, and dancing reindeers in brown and red. So taken was I by the design that she made me another in light blue, red and yellow.

One day I will get a good look at the collection, partly to clock the photographs of the models, in the hope that I might find one of those sturdy British actors, who had yet to make it big in films or on the telly.

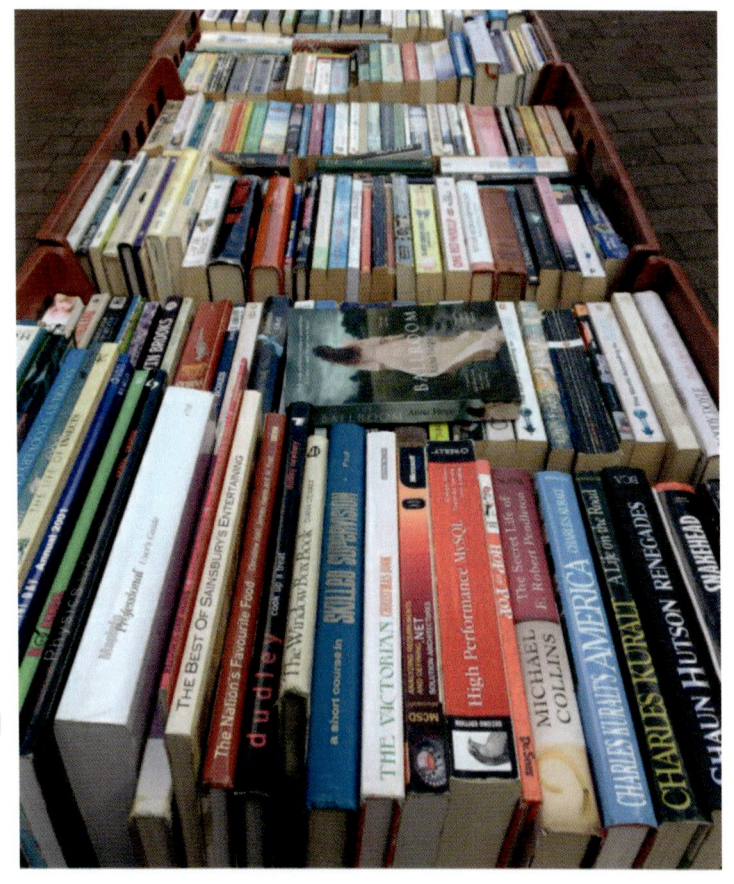

149

Highfield, numbers 2 to 18 Wilbraham Road, the shops with a secret...

everything from Mr Burt's outfitters, to Stevenson's the hair dresser, and Madame Sarah Fairhurst milliner to the best.

Now the row of shops that starts at Keppel Road and runs down to Albany is pretty typical of what you can see on

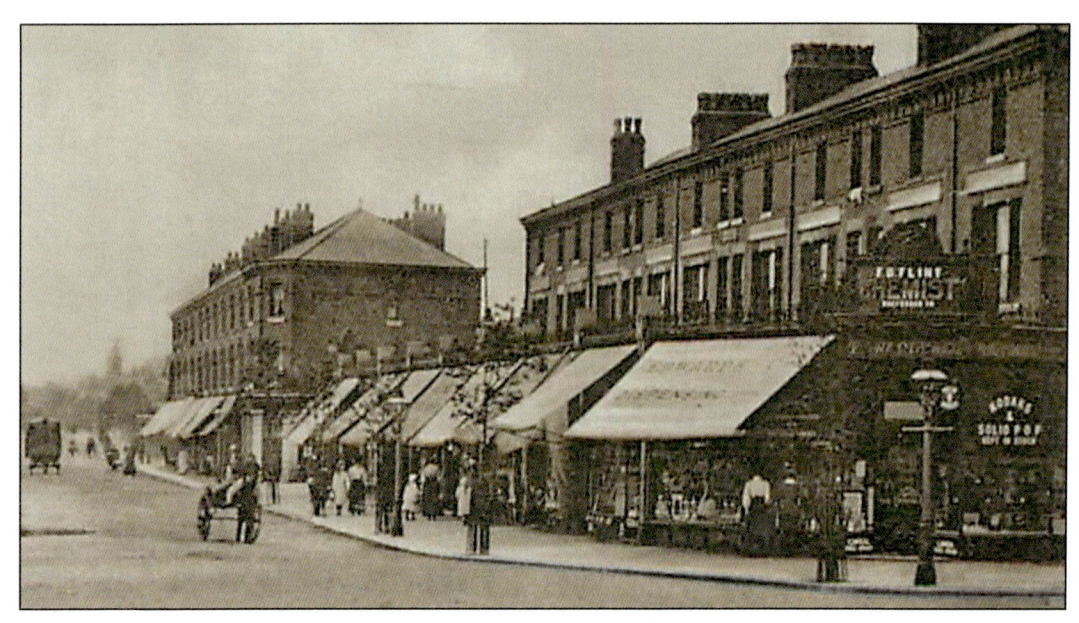

Highfield Wilbraham Road circa 1900

Wilbraham Road. There is a charity shop, four fast food outlets, a newsagent and a chemist and, if you have been round long enough, you can probably remember what each of them was before today.

But the block is a little unique in that two of the shops which traded here had done so from the beginning of the last century,

Highfield Wilbraham Road 1885

151

and only just shut up shop with the coming of the millennium. Nor is that quite all because Highfield holds another surprise, which is that the shops are a later addition to what were originally a fine row of terraced houses with neat front gardens, convenient for the railway station and Corporation tram services.

Some of the shops still retain a small staircase at the rear, which gives access to a raised floor, and once would have been the steps that led up to the front door from the garden.

The conversion was only one of a number that took place during the early 20th century. Back along Wilbraham Road, another canny developer saw the potential for more revenue, and added shops to the front of the properties which are beside Manchester Road.

Highfield may have been that bit more sought after by shop keepers, given that it was close to the station and the Post Office. Certainly both Mr Burt and Mr Stevenson thought so. The Burts set up a gentleman's outfitters' business on the corner of Wilbraham and Keppel Roads, and ran a stationer's directly opposite. Mr Stevenson also saw the potential of the new block, and moved in sometime soon after Mr Burt.

What fascinates me about Mr Stevenson, is that he not only described himself as a "hairdresser", but also was "a wig

Advert for J.R. Stevenson's 1908

maker and fancy dealer".

I have to confess that the term "fancy dealer" had me stumped, but it describes someone who sold imitation jewellery and ornaments, which in the context of the shop made perfect sense.

After all, having had your hair done for that night out, it made sense to buy something special to go with it, and no doubt Miss Emma Stevenson, who assisted in "the sales department" could be relied on to offer up expert advice.

At 27, she was 15 years younger than her brother, and may well have joined the business when Mr Stevenson made the move from his shop on Barlow Moor Road, which I think he opened in 1899.

Back then, he employed two male hairdressers, and seems to have made the move to Wilbraham Road sometime between 1903 and 1908.

Quentin Crisp on the side of a wall

So successful was the move to Highfield, that neither the Stevenson family or the Burts saw any reason to move, and continued offering perms and ties to generations of Chorlton people.

At which point, I could speculate on whether Quentin Crisp, whom we met earlier, might have visited either of the two businesses, but that would just be seen as a very obvious ruse to end with the street painting of the said Mr Crisp, on the side of Mr Burt's shop, and that would never do.

The Post Office, that letter box and a story about The Blitz...

always be careful which side of the Post Box you use.

Now it may seem daft today to be worried about posting in the wrong slot on that big pillar box by the Post Office, but I can tell you I always double checked before letting a letter drop from my hand.

Back then, and it wasn't that long ago, one slot was marked "UK Only" while the other was for the "Rest of the World".

And I often wondered what happened if you got it wrong. Would the Milan Central Post Office return my letter to me... or send it on to Aunt Edna in Derby, and would they add extra postage to cover its return trip?

Not that I ever bothered to ask in the Post Office what would happen if I posted wrongly, or for that matter why the policy seems to have changed.

I can't say I have come across many of these double pillar boxes. There was one in St Ann's Square, and I would occasionally come across them in London. They are, according to my friend David Harrop, who is an expert on all things posty, "C type pillar boxes. The first were introduced in London in the 1880s and the double apertures have been used over the years for different destinations.

The ones in London tended to have one slot for London and the other slot for the rest of the country while, more recently, one aperture was designated first class and the other second class. There was a variation which was classified the D type, which had a stamp machine on one side and, during the last world war, some were repainted with a special yellow paint which could detect gas".[1]

All of which is an introduction to our missing Post office, and the tragedy that was the Manchester Blitz.

On the night of December 24th, and into the early morning of December 25th 1940, thirty people died in Chorlton.

They were all victims of the second night of the Manchester

1 Harrop, David, October, 2017

After the Raid, what to do once the bombs have fallen 1940

Blitz, in which an estimated 644 people were killed, and another 2,000 injured.

Of the 30 who died here, many came from just two roads, while the rest were spread out across the township. Most of the bodies were taken to Withington Hospital, a few to Embden Street mortuary, and a few to the Cavendish Road [now Corkland Road] mortuary.

And I suppose it was the fact that the mortuary on Cavendish Road was just round the corner, that explains why Mr and Mrs Carr were taken there.

They lived at 549a Wilbraham Road, which took a direct hit from a high explosive bomb. Their home and two others which stood on the site of the modern post office were destroyed.[1]

I would like to write more of Ernest and Gene Carr, but so far I have only been able to turn up his death certificate, which recorded his death on that December night, and that he was

POST OFFICE, CHORLTON-CUM-HARDY.

The Post Office circa 1910

just 44 years old. It isn't much but it is a start.

So in the meantime I shall concentrate on their home and what happened on the site before and after that night.

Earlier in the century, 549a had been one of three houses which were originally numbered, 3, 5 & 7 Wilbraham Road.

They were built sometime after 1885, and were typical of the new sort of properties that were being built to meet the influx of people to Chorlton.

Many of these were professionals; a few owned their own businesses, and a lot more worked in the offices and big shops of Manchester. They were attracted here by a train service, which could whisk them into the heart of the city in under 15 minutes, and the fields, farms and open country which for many were even closer.

So, along with a surgeon and his family at number 1, the remaining three were the home at various times to a retired cotton merchant, a widow "living on her own means", Edward Ireland, who had a number of photographic studios in Manchester, and a doctor, dentist and an oil trader.

And the size of the houses reflected the inhabitants.

1 493a has been number 5 Wilbraham Road in the early of the last century

Number 1 had twelve rooms, 3 and 5 eight rooms, and number 7 had 9 rooms.

Each had cellars, a decent front garden, and a longer one at the back, stretching down across what is now the sorting office and yard.

But like other stretches of property in this new part of Chorlton, they were soon developed with the addition of shop fronts and, perhaps with an eye to even greater profits, the owners sub divided the shops.

In 1911, at number 3a there was Harvey Goodwin, confectioner, and at number 3 Mrs Ethel May, cycle dealer, while at 5a, Stuart Gray ran a tobacconist, and in number 5, C&W. Copping advertised themselves as china merchants.

Wilbraham Road circa 1885

The last of our three had become the post office in 1901, and remained so until the night of December 24th.

The Chorlton bomb maps show the impact of the high explosive bomb on the three properties, and photographs from the late 1950s show the remnant, which was the bit that jutted out still in use.

In 1959 it was being used as the Conservative Party Committee rooms, before it was demolished, and the site became the forecourt for what has variously been Lipton's, and Ethel Austin and is now a charity shop.

Now those of you keen on a bit of modern archaeology will be able to see the clue to what had happened to number 7, which is the cemented up side of what is now the gable end of the phone shop. Back in the 1950s, this was Brighter Homes, the paint and wall paper shop.

The New Post Office 1961

Any one growing up in those post war years will remember the gaps in houses, and the same raw cement walls, where part of the terrace had been demolished.

And looking at a 1959 picture, it is just possible to see the space where numbers 3 and 5 had been, which in 1961 became our new post office.

It was the obvious thing to do, to build it close to the old one and utilise the bombsite.

I did wonder whether there might have been a plaque to record the event of that night's bombing, but then, even here in Chorlton, there would have been plenty of candidates for such a memorial.

And at the time, there would have been plenty who remembered the event and maybe even knew Ernest and Gene Carr.

But what was once a common experience is fast passing out of living memory, and soon I doubt that any one will even pass a thought to the odd space that runs from the Gable Nook Nursery, to the row of shops by the bus stop.

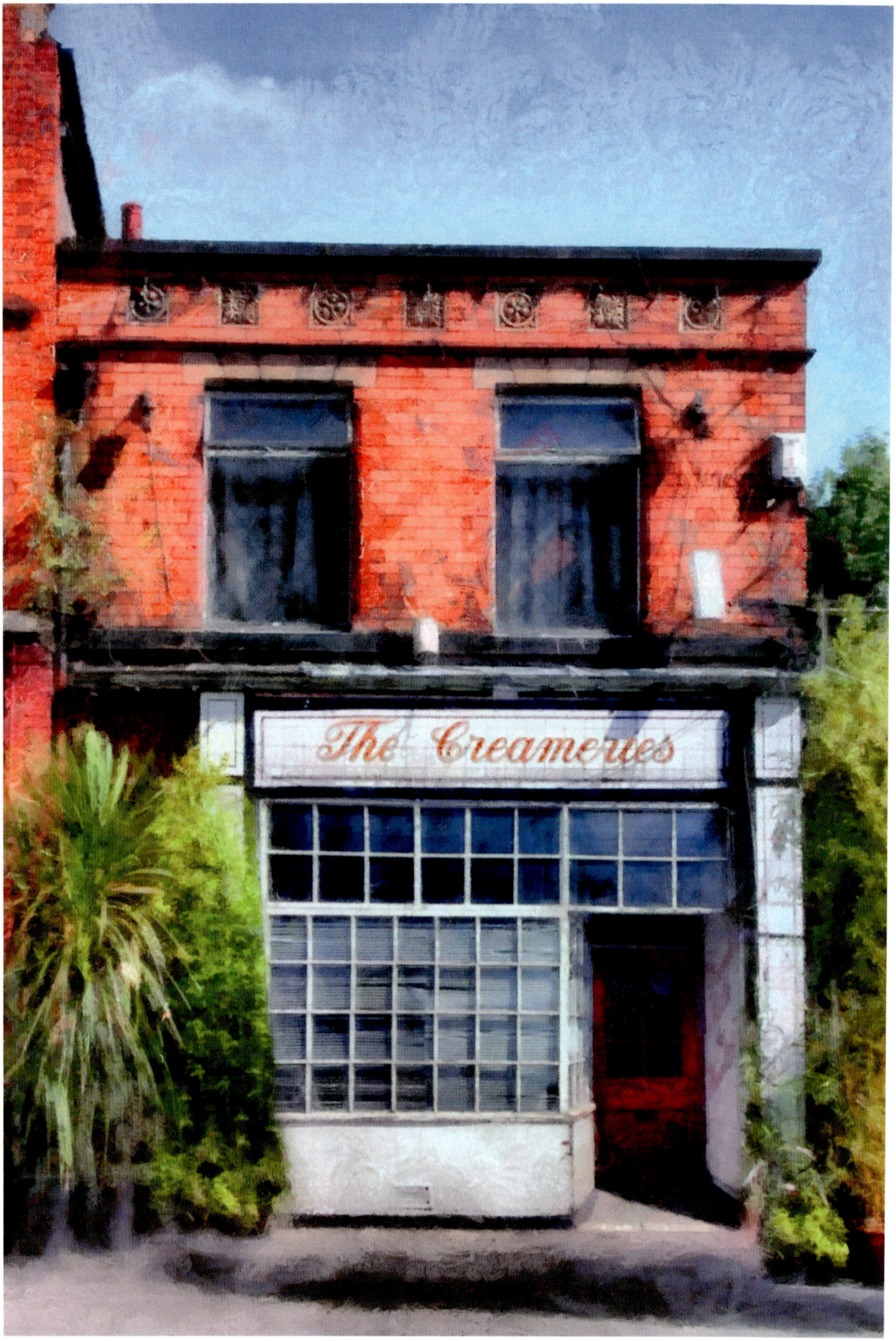
The Creameries

Over the railway bridge, past the Egerton Arcade and then to the Creameries…
a new venture with a sideways glance at our traditions.

The curious tourist may well ask why there are so many references to the Egerton family, whether it be Egerton Road North and Egerton Road South, the Egerton Arcade, or Wilbraham Road, which was also named after a family member.

The answer is of course, the Egerton estate once owned much of the land in Chorlton, as well as great chunks of the rest of south Manchester. At which point I should also mention the Lloyd Estate, which also got in on the act, and bought land in Chorlton in the 18th century.

None of which has much to do with Creameries, other than that the shop stands next to the Egerton Arcade.

Before the widespread use of refrigerators, most people bought their diary produce fairly frequently. If you were lucky enough to live near a farm which had its own creamery, then you bought your milk, butter and cheese from them. And there are still people who remember being sent to Riley's at Ivy Green Farm on Beech Road, to buy milk.

The old farmhouse on the Green, which had been in the hands of the Higginbotham family from the 1840s, still has its creamery, which faces north, as it should do, to ensure it is the coldest part of the cottage.

But, away from the Green and as the area north of the old village was developed in the last decades of the 19th century, there were creameries on Barlow Moor Road, and here on Wilbraham Road. Walter, who used to live on Acres Road, once told me that he had begun work as a boy of 14, at a creamery on Railway Terrace, at the junction of Buckingham and Manchester Roads.

Now there is a lot more work to do to date the Creamery. It was established

"Drink Milk for Health"

sometime after 1911, but as yet, I can't give a definite date. Out of curiosity, I asked the previous owners of the shop if there was anything left of the old creamery, but sadly there was nothing.

But like all good stories, this one has a happy ending, because what was once a Creamery will be so again, although there is a slight twist to the tale. According to Sophie, one of the team at the Creameries, "it's a bakery and that's the core. What we're serving could be as simple as a piece of bread and butter, but it's a treat, and truly delicious.

"Key to our menu is bread, cheese, wine and beer. The baker's oven is the focal point of The Creameries, and our baked dishes go perfectly with our lines in house cheese, butter and cured meats.

"Our aim is to create intelligent and thoughtful food that keeps people happy and interested. We will emphasise British cooking and food provenance, working with ethically minded suppliers.

"The team consists of Mary Ellen McTague, who is in charge of menus, drinks and service, Sophie Yeoman, who will be working full time in the kitchen and managing the site, and Soo Wilkinson who is on charge of interior design, marketing and events.

"The Creameries should open in March of 2018".

And that I think is a nice way to conclude... with a new venture which is different, but which retains something of the old Chorlton.

The Creameries Wilbraham Road 1960

ALL OF FAME
Being a collection of those who have lived still live or passed through Chorlton.

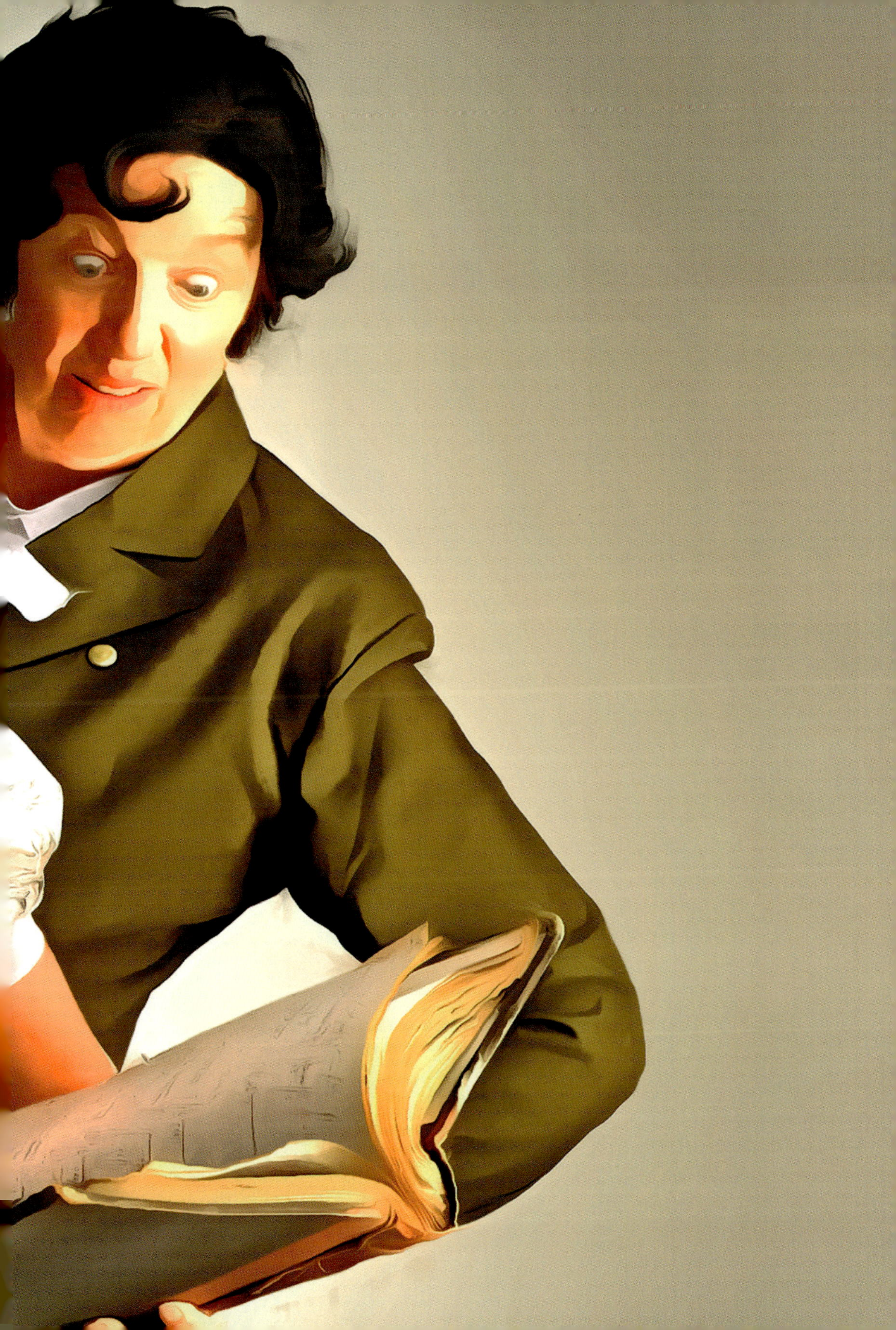

Cosgrove Hall building was next to Unicorn

Somewhere in the deepest recesses of where we live will be the offices of the 'Committee for the Preservation and Promotion of Significant Chorlton Residents' which has as part of its mission statement "the ongoing task of identifying individuals who, in their daily lives, have lifted the spirits and brought a smile to the people of the district".

And if that Committee doesn't exist, it jolly well should, and so with that thought in mind our last chapter is dedicated to those who have lived here, still live here or passed through.

There is no hard and fast rule about who qualifies for being on the list and I bet there will be some we have omitted or not done justice to in someone's opinion. But the list which is a long one, has been suggested by friends, colleagues and family, allowing us to abrogate any responsibility for those we included and even more for those we didn't. The pantheon of Chorlton's A list appears in the footnotes in no particular order and we have mixed real and stage names of celebrities, and included some who remain in the imagination of their creators.[1] The fun, should you choose to take part in it, is to discover what you can of those we just mention and come back to us with other names for consideration and inclusion in part two of the Quirks of Chorlton.

Unlike the other chapters in the book, there is no map to guide your travels. Peter's cartography skills are indeed well up to the task, but the individuals in question are so far spread out around Chorlton that he map would take the form of one of those fold out ones, and we all know how almost impossible they are to get back into the neatly folded space.

Eric suggested a variation which was a long roll map, but Helen pointed out that it would not fit easily on the coffee table or in the satchel.

But I am convinced that the enterprising reader will rise above such mild inconsistencies and sally forth across the district armed with an A to Z or one of those old fashioned bus timetables which provided easy to read little maps.

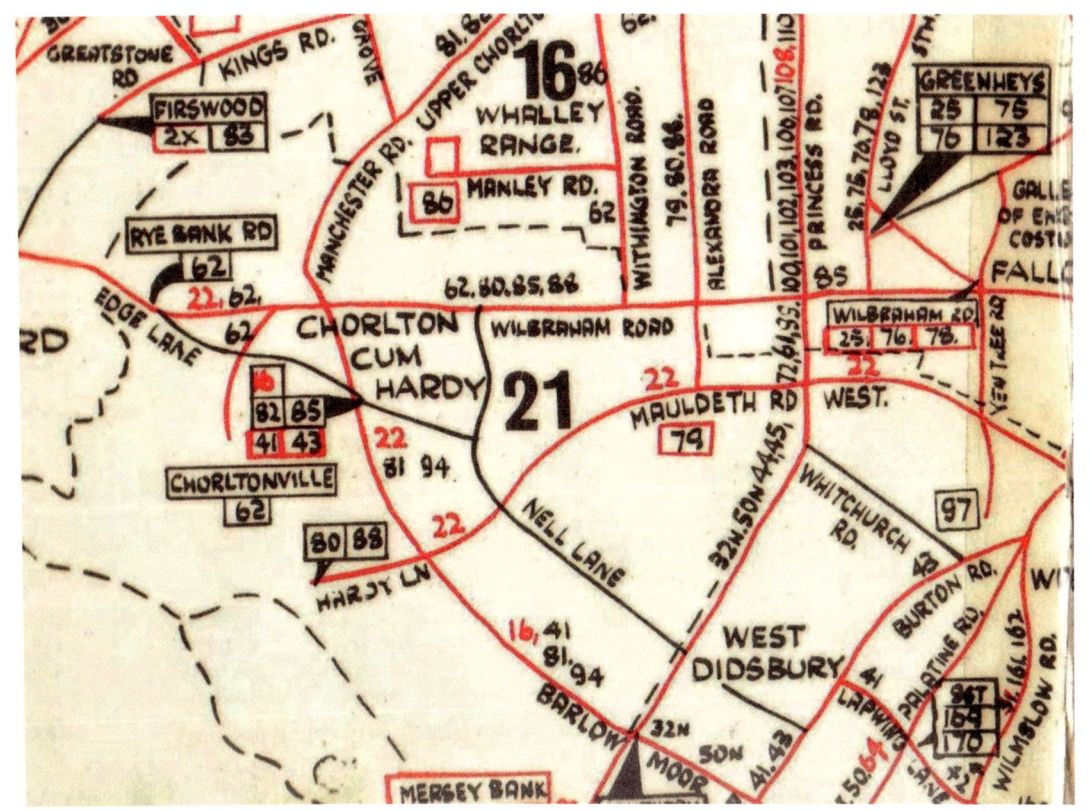

Travel by bus through Chorlton 1963

1 Doris Speed, Kevin Kennedy aka Curly Watts, Ken Barlow, Morrissey, Stone Roses, Danger Mouse, Chorlton and the Wheelies, Bob The Builder created, at the animation powerhouse Cosgrove Hall, Mick Hucknall, Peter Barlow, David Threlfall, Jason Mansford, Denis Law, Elbow, Warren Clark.

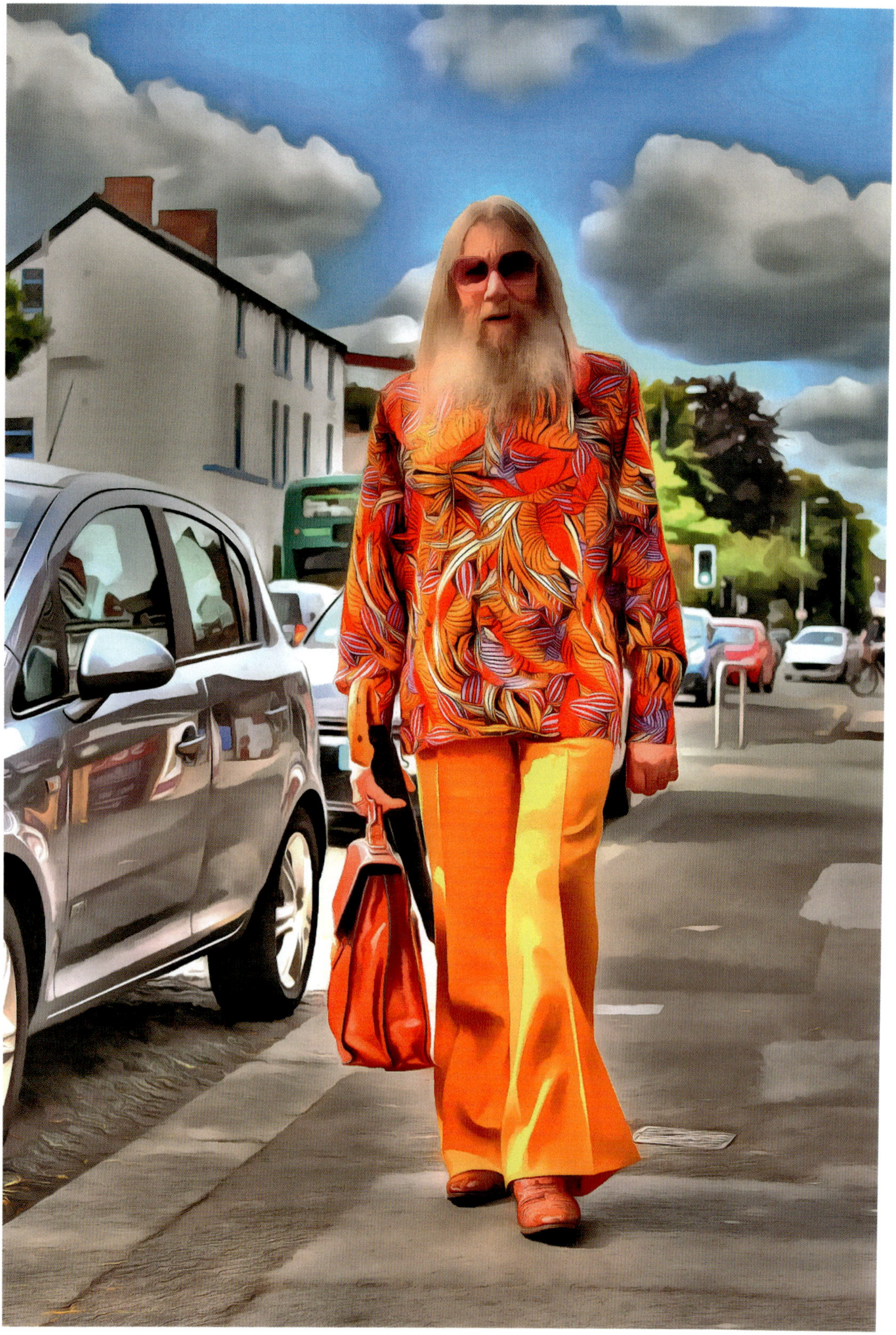

Alan Hollingum...

the man who isn't what everyone thinks.

Now many readers will be familiar with Alan who dresses well and who in his time has been mistaken for a University professor and a leading member of a '70s rock group and who has been around Chorlton for over 40 years.

Alan recently referred to the confusion: "Musician, Artist, and University professor. These are some of the things I have never been but have often been taken to be. In truth I am a retired teacher who has lived in Chorlton since 1973. That was when I moved into a bed sitter in Warwick Road in a house owned by Bobby Barnes, the peroxide blond tag partner of TV wrestler Adrian Street.

My style is probably the only thing most people know about me. I have had a beard since 1962, flared trousers since 1968, all-year-round sunglasses since 1972, mid-calf length double breasted overcoats since 1975 and colourful silk shirts; all made the same way since 1981.

It's the best I can make of myself so I shall stick with it while I can. Others will make of it what they will".

And others do speak fondly of Alan whose appearance always cheers them up, be it at the bus stop on a wet day in February or across the table of one of our coffee shops.

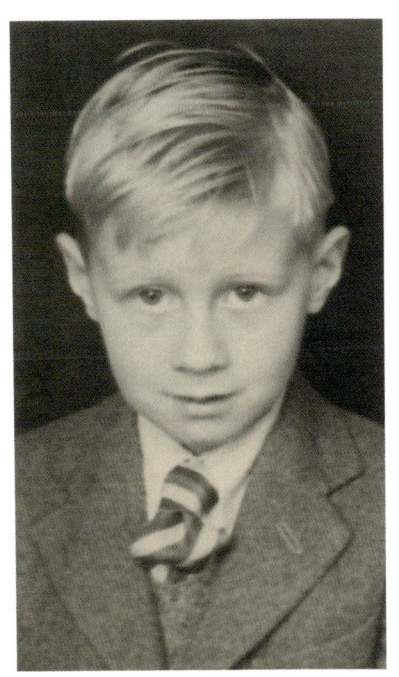

Alan at Junior School 1953

July 2015 Photo © Robert Walker

Joe Mercer, the letter helping him with his team selection and other notable football chaps...

"Dear Mr Mercer about the team for this Saturday's game..."

Last month I found my old football boots, which were third hand when I got them in 1961. They were all brown leather and served me well for four years before organised sport and I parted company. But looking at them all over again was to be reminded of how the beautiful game has moved on.

I grew up with stories of friends who travelled on buses to matches with their sporting heroes, exchanging the odd story of past games and of bumping into them on Saturday nights outside the local pub.

In the case of the young Tony Goulding, it was St John's Church on High Lane which both he and Sir Matt Busby attended.

And Chorlton has had its fair share of soccer celebrities, with Dennis Law living on Claude Road, George Best and David Sadler in "digs" off Mersey Bank and the managers of Man' United and Man' City residing respectively on Kings Road and St Werburghs Road.

Back then, the link between the lives of managers, players and supporters was less remote and so it was perfectly sensible for a young fan to write to the manager of a football team with suggestions on who should be selected for the next game.

One day I will ask Tony the full story behind the letter he sent to Joe Mercer who was the manager of Tony's beloved Manchester City and whether he delivered it by hand or sent it

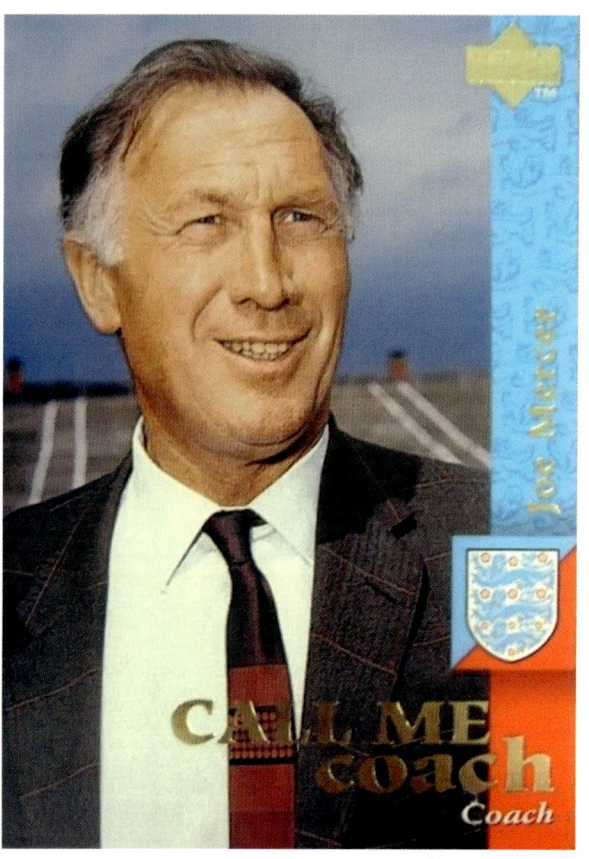

Joe Mercer 1999

through the post, but I do know that Mr Mercer didn't reply.

But to be fair, I suspect that there might have been a fair few such letters falling through the letterbox of that house on St Werburgh's Road on any day of the week during the season.

And at the other end of the game, Chorlton, over the last century and a bit, has had quite a few amateur teams, of which my favourite must be Chorlton Albion. I came across the team when Ann Love told me about her family connection to the Albion in the 1920s.

Tony's letter to Mr Mercer circa 1960s

Her dad played for them and, just to prove they existed, she sent me some team pictures, lists of fixtures and a set of postcards inviting the players to away matches.

This was pretty much at the extent of my knowledge so I asked Lawrence who is a font of knowledge and who told me, "The early years of 20th Century saw the appearance of several football clubs in the suburbs, some short-lived. Chorlton Albion's home pitch was on the corner of Hardy Lane and Barlow Moor Road, near where the Co-op is now".[1]

And added "details about defunct football clubs at this level are patchy at best. It throws up questions of were there any changing facilities, what fixtures did they play and in what colours?"

Leaving me to report that Chorlton Albion appear to have played Stalybridge Celtic AFC on a regular basis and, using the away match postcards, it was possible to track the opponents to Mottram Road where they still play today. And that in turn raises the question of just how they would get there back in the 1920s.

1 Beadle Lawrence, 2016

Chorlton Albion 1925 colourised with an imagined strip

171

Allan with dad circa 1940s

Allan Brown and a century of the Chorlton Brass Band...

"A quiet unassuming chap with a box full of stories about Chorlton whose connection with our Brass Band went back more than seventy years".

It is odd to think that we had a brass band which was one of the oldest brass bands in the country, having been started in the 1820s.

Of course the Stalybridge Band is older and can claim to have marched in to St Peter's Fields on the day of Peterloo, but ours had an almost continuous run until it agreed to wind up after the last world war.

It performed in many of the great and not so great events here in the township and went on to win prizes in brass band competitions.

In its early days, it consisted of 24 members, most of whom were agricultural workers and had to rely on funds raised through subscriptions or from gifts from local benefactors like Samuel Mendle who, until his trading business with the Far East collapsed, was a wealthy contributor.

But there was also more than a bit of "self help" and, in the case of James Axon, this meant making his own drum which was fine, but when finished proved too large to get out through the door of his cottage.

The band also reflected the changing nature of Chorlton,

Chorlton Brass Band 1893

Allan sometime in the 1930s

so, while in the 1820s it was mainly drawn from those engaged in farming who had been born here and whose families had lived here for generations, by the 1890s, many band members were new to the area, having been born elsewhere or whose parents had moved into Chorlton.

And in the seventy or so years since the band began, the occupations of the players had changed, reflecting that big change which saw Chorlton move from a rural community to a suburb of Manchester. So by the 1890s many of the band made their living from clerical jobs, or working in warehouses.

And the key that offered up the information on those changes was contained in a photograph of the band performing at Barlow Hall in 1893. It is a picture which will be familiar to many but on the copy owned by my friend Allan Brown were the names of the men who played that day.

And as every historian will tell you, with a name and a date, it is possible to pursue each individual through a variety of official documents, letters, and memories.

So I owe Allan a lot, and not only for the band picture, but because he shared his large collection of photographs of Chorlton with me.

Many of our conversations started with a name or an event and, in the course of the afternoon, we would wander over everything from Chorlton's Brass band, to his early years in the school on the Green and his memories of his grandmother who laid out the dead.

But he was never one to think he knew it all and was forever asking me about my latest bit of research and, more often than not, that in turn led back to an Allan story.

So it was with the barrage balloon on the Rec which my old dog walking friend John Telford first told me about over thirty years ago, even pointing out where the concrete base was to be found.

Then one day this tiny bit of wartime history was taken away during a refurbishment of the recreation ground and, bit by bit, I came to doubt my own memory but Allan had the picture of the balloon along with a story.

But it is his pictures of the brass band that intrigued me.

Of these, my own favourite was of the band, possibly in the 1920s, behind the old school. It includes Allan's grandfather, and a young girl looking over the wall at what all the fuss was about.

My regret is that we didn't pursue the research into his own family which got so far but was interrupted by other projects and then, when I was ready to start, he had died.

His cousin Philip remembers that, "Allan was most particular about the spelling of his name. His first name was William but he seldom used it except on official documents. He

Chorlton Brass Band 1930s

had a close friendship with the author, Eddie Johnson, who has written many extremely detailed books about this region's railways and who used Allan's formidable library of photos to illustrate his books.

Eddie maintained that Allan was, 'the finest holder of railway information and his knowledge was unique.'

Allan always insisted on the use of his full initials in the acknowledgements, which would appear as WAB. He was very pleased and honoured when one of his photos was used as an illustration on the information board of St. Werburgh's tram station platform and, of course, acknowledged WAB!

But I have been musing on the spelling of Allan's name and done a little ferreting around with the help of my sister who has Allan's birth certificate. On this document he is named as 'William Alan Brown' and I have since recalled that he determined that he would rename himself 'Allan' in his early teenage years in homage to Ian Allan, the author of the ultimate aid to locomotive fans everywhere.

"In our conversation you mentioned that his grandmother laid out dead bodies".

This is perfectly true and it is the case that Allan, for many years, used a redundant coffin lid from her time as a layer outer as his ironing board! My sister, Joan and I found it in the outdoor shed after his death. I believe my sister may well have it as a memento because it is a prime example of the 'quirky' nature of the man".

I might add that Allan had inherited a huge collection of stuffed animals from his mother and, at one time, these stretched down the long passageway from the front door and also took over the living room.

Never one to be sentimental about such things, Allan disposed of them each week in the Corporation bin and my sister Joan found one, a stag's head, when she spotted an antler protruding from the bin. It was always a matter of regret to her that she was unable to save the rest.

During the time I knew him, Allan was working to get young people involved with brass bands at a local high school and, along with other members of Chorlton Good Neighbours, shared his memories of an older Chorlton with students at Brookburn School.[1]

His knowledge and anecdotes about the district could be amusing and informative and were never dull and he will be missed by many.

Allan Brown 1928-2015.

Allan at Brookburn School 2011

1 Chorlton Good Neighbours, https://chorltongoodneighbours.org/ Wilbraham St Ninians Church, Egerton Road South, Chorlton-cum-Hardy, Manchester M21 0XJ, Tel: 0161 881 2925

Stephen Raw, that £2 coin and a map of Gondor...

the artist from London who said to all his friends he'd be back in 36 weeks and 40 years later is still in Chorlton.

    It is one of those familiar stories of people who have made Chorlton their home, having never really planned to stay.

    Stephen Raw is a textual artist who told Peter "I began my career producing 'bespoke' lettering and calligraphy for book covers - lots of different styles for a wide range of fiction and poetry. I did maps as well and had produced some for an African journey book when the Tolkien editors wanted new maps for 'The Lord of the Rings'. I drew the 'Shire' map first which Christopher Tolkien, the son, liked as I had kept enough of his quirky lettering while making it much more legible. So I got the commission to draw them all, which took me about a year off and on".

Stephen also carried the title of 'Lettering Consultant to Her Majesty, Queen Elizabeth II', because for ten years he served on the Mint's Design Advisory Committee, and while he no longer discharges that responsibility, he was invited to submit designs for various circulating coins. One design was accepted and the coin will be released in 2018, but he is bound by that most secret of oaths not to say anymore on the matter.

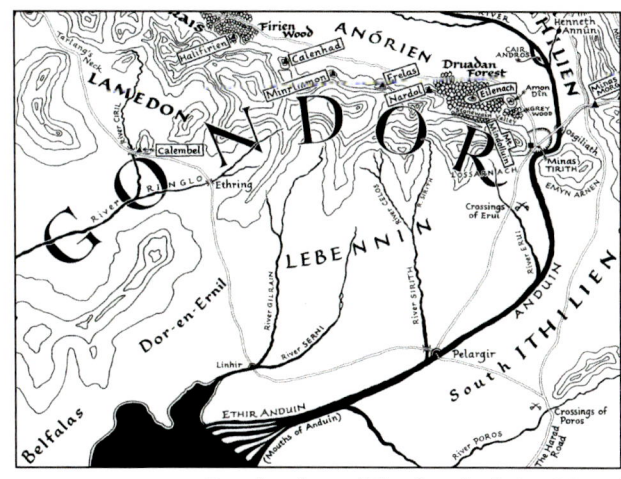

Gondor from 'The Lord of the Rings'

That said, I can reveal that it is his lettering that appears on some of our coins, for example on the Magna Carta £2 coin, and he also designed that stained glass window at the old Macfadyn's Church on the corner of Barlow Moor and Zetland Roads, along with a recent commission for Manchester Cathedral.

All of which just leaves me to reveal that he came to Manchester to do an MA at the Poly, having told friends in London that "I'd be back in 36 weeks time. 40-odd years later I still haven't made the journey back south".

My aunt and uncle were living in Chandos Road and I stayed with them before moving to a flat nearby, and after living in Moss Side and Papua New Guinea, returned to Chorlton".

Calligraphy for the Magna Carta £2 coin

179

Kingbee records and a wealth of musical talent...

from a stall by the post office to the shop which is home to thousands of new and used records and CDs, covering all musical tastes.

Now it is not much of a leap from our own Brass Band to Kingbee Records and a host of musical talent that has been associated with Chorlton.

The list includes Damon Gough, alias Badly Drawn Boy, who made Chorlton his home, The Bee Gees who lived on Keppel Road, went to Oswald Road School and performed in the old cinema on Manchester Road, and Morrissey who wrote about Whalley Range. And to this you can add The Stone Roses, along with Guy Garvey of Elbow, who reportedly slipped on an avocado while walking through Chorlton, and heaps of new musicians who regularly perform in the local bars and the Arts Festival.

But if you are of a certain generation who wanted to be like Sandra Dee or played skiffle and argued about whether Elvis, Tommy Steele or Marty Wilde was the best, then the Bee Gees will always have a special place.

The Bee Gees and the cover of Saturday Night Fever LP 1977

Their first band included a tea chest base which, as every skiffle fan will know, was a cheap and essential accompaniment to the guitars and drum and was the mainstay of Skiffle music.

But the Bee Gees moved on and, during the late 1960s, released a succession of successful records, while composing for some of the best known British and American singers. At the end of the next decade and into the 80s, they changed direction and a whole new generation knew them as the men who did the sound track for Saturday Night Fever.

Nor has it stopped there, with the Bee Gees reaching out to new audiences that cross the decades. So many of those at the 2017 Glastonbury Festival who applauded Barry Gibb during his solo performance hadn't been born when John Travolta bounced across the screen to the sound of Night Fever, and I suspect nor had their parents met when the Bee Gees recorded To Love Somebody.

Badly Drawn Boy Live at l'Elysée Montmartre © Claude-Étienne Armingaud

Not bad for the lads from Keppel Road.

By contrast, while Damon Gough was not born here, Chorlton is where he chose to live.

I remain hopeful that I might just bump into him at some point if only to ask about the origins of the name Badly Drawn Boy. And yes I know the story of the inspiration for the name from a character in Sam and His Magic Ball, but it is always nice to pick up on the subtle nuances and perhaps point out that the said animation programme was made by Cosgrove

Hall which as everyone knows was based in Chorlton.

And that could give me an opportunity to mention Danger Mouse and the Chorlton Wheelies, but here I fear I am off message and will leave the story of Cosgrove Hall, and Danger Mouse to another time, although I know that Eric remains convinced that all the characters in Danger Mouse, including Penfold, Colonel K, Baron Silas Greenback along with Stiletto Mafiosa, Leatherhead and Nero were all modelled on people he knew.

And somewhere in one of the stories must be a record shop which is another of those impossible links that by degrees lead us to King Bee Records,

But, before that, there was Nightingale's at 436 Wilbraham

Nightingale's on Wilbraham Road 1960

1 Kingbee Records, 519, Wilbraham Road, 0161 860 4762, www.kingbeerecords.co.uk/

Road, which sold all things electrical and, by 1960, had an impressive range of televisions, transistor radios, fridges and washing machines in its window.

It was there by 1938 and still there in 1960 and there is in the collection one old 78 RPM record of the Boston Promenade Orchestra performing the Ritual Fire Dance and the Conclusion to Bolero conducted by Arthur Fiedler.

The catalogue number dated the record to 1938, while the perfectly preserved dust cover offered up the Nightingale name and the address of both the Chorlton shop and another at 58 Wilmslow Road in Withington.

At which point I can claim little credit for the find or much of the subsequent research.

It was Andy Robertson's son who came across the record and Andy who went looking in Manchester's digital collection for images of the shop in the 1960s, leaving me the easy job

All that was electrical in the window of Nightingale's in 1960

of hunting down the record in the HMV catalogue.

In time, I am sure there will be people who offer up all sorts of memories of the shop, what they bought there and perhaps a beginning and end date to the business.

For now, I shall just reflect that it wasn't too long ago that high streets and humbler parades of shops could boast a full range of shopping experiences from the wool shop, electrical business along with DIY, hardware and the odd travel agents.

Record sleeve 1938

So there you have it - a bit of our consumer past on Wilbraham Road, with just one last observation that Nightingale's had gone by 1969.

But just eighteen years later and a little further down Wilbraham Road, Kingbee Records started selling their unique take on all things musical.

The shop is owned by Les Hare who opened for business in 1986 with a stall in the building which is now the charity shop next to the post office. Three months later, he moved to the present site at 519 Wilbraham Road. Those first three months were not without incident and Les remembers the day when a friend who was looking after the business played the Smith's song, "Meat is murder" which did not go down too well with the butcher opposite.

I remember the first time I came across the shop, which must have been soon after it opened, and lost any sense of time as I went from one favourite section to another.

Now that we have lost so many of those other quirky shops like Bryan the Book, Keith Allen's furniture shop and Kingspot, it is good to be able to buy books at Chorlton Bookshop and music from Kingbee Records.

185

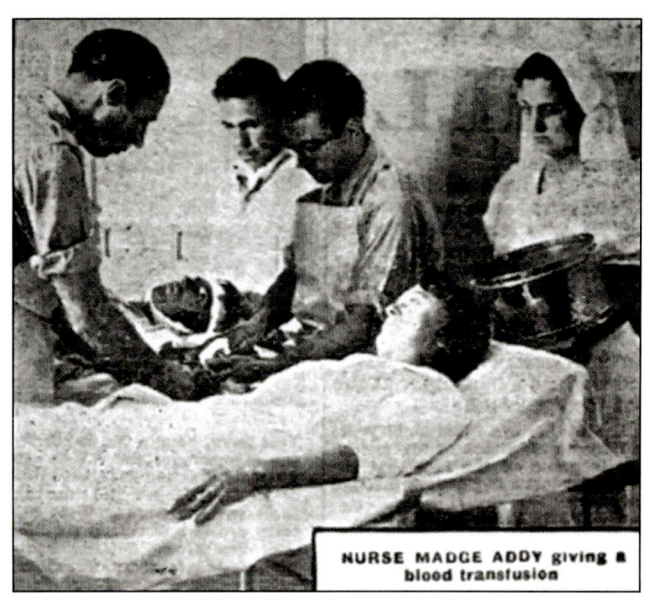

NURSE MADGE ADDY giving a blood transfusion

The Daily Worker 1938

Spain Fights for Independence 1936-39

Madge Addy, a remarkable woman...

"Saving life by giving her own blood is just a casual affair to Nurse Madge Addy while serving in the Spanish Civil War".

Madge Addy was a remarkable woman whom history and Chorlton have forgotten.

According to one source, she was "from the Chorlton-cum-Hardy area of Manchester and arrived in Spain in 1937, becoming Head Nurse at a hospital in an old monastery at Uclés in Castile. Like some of the other British nurses, she was also involved with the fund-raising campaigns back home".[1]

Madge would write detailed letters about the work being done in the 'Manchester Ward' at the hospital in Uclés to the Chairman of the North Manchester Spanish Medical Aid Committee to help with the campaigns for medical supplies.

The letters and articles give vivid descriptions of the revenge carried out by the victorious forces of Franco on the civil population and those who sided with the defeated democratic government of Spain.

And she was the last British nurse to leave Spain.

During the Second World War, she was in Occupied France and played a vital role in setting up the famous 'Garrow-Pat O'Leary' escape line, working with MI9.

She was awarded the OBE for her work, and her bravery included travelling as a Norwegian subject on German civil flights, carrying secret messages sewn into the lining of her fur coat.

As an English woman operating in enemy-occupied territory, she would have known what the penalty would be if caught. Madge Addy died in 1970".[2]

Like all good stories I came across it by chance after Cllr Shelia Newman of Chorlton had been asked to look into the possibility of erecting a plaque to the memory of Ms Addy.

The cost will be met by voluntary subscriptions which just leaves a decision on its location.

She had been born in Fallowfield but worked in a hairdressing business on Manchester Road in Chorlton just before she left for Spain.

Her activities have been largely forgotten and neither the Guardian nor the Times carried an obituary when she died in 1970.

But this is now being rectified by Chris Hall who has not only been researching her life but is working towards the erection of a blue plaque. Anyone wanting to help with the campaign should contact Chris whose detail are in the footnotes.[3]

Aid for the Basque Heroes 1936-39

1 Jackson, Angela, From foodships to the front lines: a forgotten Manchester heroine of the Spanish Civil War
2 Ibid, Jackson, Angela,
3 Chris by email at christoff_hall@yahoo.com or on 0161 861 7448.

Stan, Mona, Chris and Lyn, at the Trevor...
pulling pints and making us happy for almost a quarter of a century.

    I suppose we all have our favourite pubs and publicans.

    For me it will always be Stan and Mona of the Trevor and their two daughters Chris and Lyn.

    It was a welcoming place and one where, even if you were on your own, there were always people you could sit with, pass the time and have a jolly good natter, helped, of course, by pints from the bar.

    And, as ever, it is those behind that bar that set the tone, and in the case of Stan, Mona and the girls they ran a happy place.

Stan and Mona had taken over the Trevor in 1955 and continued to pull pints until 1979. On a Friday and Saturday, the pub was heaving and there were times when it seemed so crowded that you were gently transported down the lounge just by the movement of the crowd around you.

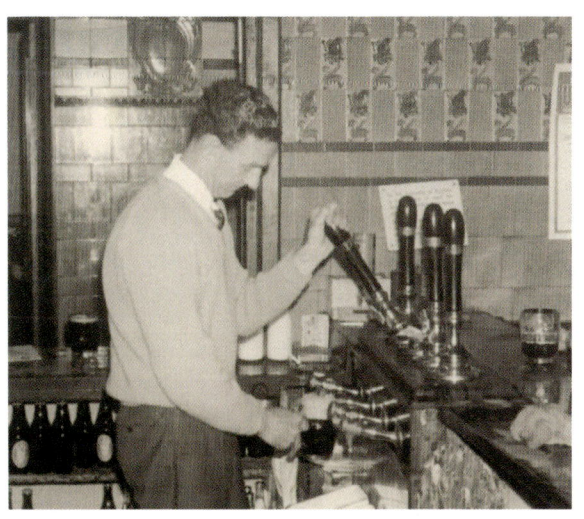

But however busy the place was, you always got served quickly, with Stan, Mona, Chris

Stan circa 1960s

and Lyn working that professional approach of starting at the two ends of the bar and moving into the middle and back out again. Of course, if you were a local you would catch the eye of the staff quicker, but there was a fairness

Mona circa 1960s

to how they worked it and that made for a happy pub.

All of this and more came flooding back to me as I sat with Lyn, Chris and Peter looking at old photographs and talking about the Trevor in the years when they were growing up.

In the space of an hour, I discovered a long forgotten picture of me from 1979, Peter heard Lyn ring the old bell for last orders which had been last heard in the pub 38 years ago and both of us were given an insight into what the pub was like soon after it had opened.

Back then and well into the 1960s, the living room and kitchen were downstairs at the back of the pub, the saloon was known as the Singing Room and once, a very long time ago,

The Bell 2017

Andrew, Jack, Mike and Tom 1979

there had been a door down the alleyway beside the chapel which was for off sales.

During those early years when Stan and Mona ran the pub, the interior with its old glazed tiles and wooden beams was pretty much as it had been when the doors opened for the first time in 1908. Stan, keeping up with the mood for all things new, took those old wooden beams and covered them with tiny squares of mirror glass.

But the long passageway from the entrance demarcating the Vault from the Singing Room remained until the modernization of the mid 60s and that demarcation allowed the rooms to be more isolated, so allowing one rogue of a chap to pursue a variety of schemes which, at best, just stopped short of being illegal but more often than not could have landed him up in prison.

For Chris and Lyn, all of this was taken for granted, along with the knife sharpening man who always set up his hand driven wheel outside the pub and, in the course of sharpening the knives, set the family dog off barking, much to Stan's displeasure, who may have muttered darkly about "the opposition" persuading the knife man to work outside the Trevor.

And, as happens in the ebb and flow of conversations long lost, memories came flooding back - like the day Tommy Steele called in at the pet shop which had been a beer shop, was to become a bakery and is now a gift and jewellery shop. According to Chris, it was around 1956-57 and Stan and the family were alerted to what was happening by the noise from Tommy Steel's fans wanting to get a glance of their idol who was inside trying to buy a monkey. I am not sure if Mr Jones who ran the pet shop had the monkey. I suspect he may have been more interested in the next visit from the Bone Man. Unlike pet shops today, Mr Jones offered an extra service which was the humane disposal of loved animals.

Having received the said pet, he would put them in a specially designed box and feed in a lethal dose, leaving his son Bob to hand over the remains to the Bone Man who made regular calls.

All of which just leaves me to return to the Trevor and remember Jim Lloyd, who was an artist, a teacher and one of our historians and who, on occasion, worked behind the public bar with Lyn and her dad and painted a sign for the pub which had pride of place on the wall of the Singing Room.

Mr Lloyd was only one of the bar staff and back in the '50s the Trevor employed 6 waiters at busy times.

After Stan and Mona left, we lingered on, but the place was not the same and, after a decent interval, we decamped, but I have never forgotten the time when they had stewardship of the Trevor and judging by many people I talk to, there are lots of people with fond memories of the pub and especially Stan, Mona, Chris and Lyn.

Stan and Mona circa 1960s

Withering Looks first shown in 1989 and still going strong © Doug Currie

LipService...

"original comedies from a distinctly female perspective since 1985".

It is a simple observation, but an important one, that we should all learn something new every day and if there is a smile or laugh to accompany it so much the better.

And it was as I was finishing my bit of the book in advance of Peter doing the clever bits with images, paintings and laying out the finished product, that I came across LipService who live in Chorlton.

To be honest it was Peter who introduced me to Maggie Fox and Sue Ryding who make up the team of LipService and their bizarre take on life.

They met as Drama students at Bristol University in a "very

serious Ibsen production of The Lady from The Sea, which had the audience on the floor laughing".

Now that would have been a production I would love to have seen, if only because, and here, I admit a prejudice, I don't like Ibsen. He is one of those playwrights you would never invite to your grandma's 90th birthday. His little piece on the joys of being 90 would be shot through with heavy and meaningful angst, and I bet most of us would instead call for LipService, who have been making people laugh since 1985. During this time, they have produced 20 original comedies for the stage, performed on Radios 2 and 4, as well as the telly, and toured the UK, Pakistan, the USA, Eastern Europe and Germany while the Independent, described them as "Britain's favourite literary lunatics", which is more than any one has said about me or Peter.

Knit One Murder One 1992 © Doug Currie

Maggie and Sue were some of the first women to be part of a new comedy movement in the eighties called Alternative Cabaret, which was a move away from the sexist, racist, homophobic, "mother-in-law" jokes.

They played the Edinburgh Festival every year, winning awards on the way for Knit One Murder One and for Withering Looks, which was perhaps one of their most popular shows, and their latest show Mr Darcy Loses the Plot is a huge success, playing to packed houses around the country.

Mr Darcy Loses the Plot 2016/2017 © Doug Currie

The Epilogue

Of Telecom Eddy, Jean the Post and the Corporation Tram terminus

There will be many people and buildings which have "missed the bus" and not been included.

One of my favourites is the old GPO building at the bottom of Keppel Road which some will think of as ugly, but I maintain is a fine example of simple functionality with those large arched windows and solid appearance.

And of course, there will also be plenty of Chorlton characters who could have but didn't slide onto the page.

But, rather than apologise for the omissions, I will close with a reflection on those nicknames for some who made it in and others who didn't.

All the way up from the playground, most of us have encountered "that one" who generates and retains a nickname. For me it was Paul Driver who fell into the baths fully clothed after a school swimming lesson in 1961 and for ever after was known as Dribble.

Some, like Bryan Barlow, to whom I referred as "Bryan the Book", need no explanation given that Bryan ran the second hand book shop on Beech Road which was a cornucopia of treasures. Jean the Post and Telecom Eddy I knew from the Trevor, and their affectionate nicknames derived from their jobs, while Scotch Ken described perfectly his favoured drink.

Of course, there will be many more who never acquired that nickname but are fondly remembered and that seems a good point to finish with just a side acknowledgement to Lewis Carroll who in 1872 wrote "When I use a word," Humpty Dumpty said, in rather a scornful tone, "it means just what I choose it to mean—neither more nor less."

And, following the logic of that utterance, I will just say that History and all things past are what we want them to be, which rather means that Telecom Eddy, the lost pond of Beech Road and The Twilight Sleep Home are subjects as valid to read about as any battle, any politician or the inventor of that non stick beer mat.

So we commend this volume of all things quirky, confident in the knowledge that a few will disagree with our choices, some will mutter "well I never knew that" and many will demand a second edition.

Manchester and the Great War

A new book by Andrew Simpson which draws on a vast collection of material never before seen. Including letters, official documents, photographs, and a wealth of everyday objects, which include picture postcards, souvenirs and very personal family memorials dedicated to all those who died in action.

Available in all good book stores.

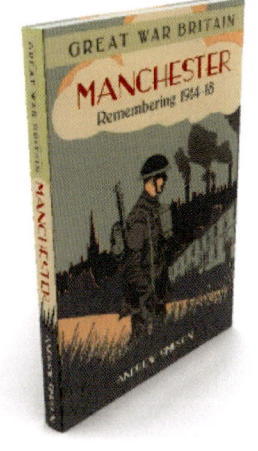

Paintings from Pictures

All the paintings that appear in this book are available to buy either on 7mm white painted MDF board with a brush stroke varnish finish or as an A3 giclee print.

For further information get in touch with Peter by email at peter@paintingsfrompictures.co.uk or Telephone 07521 557888

Other Books by The Authors

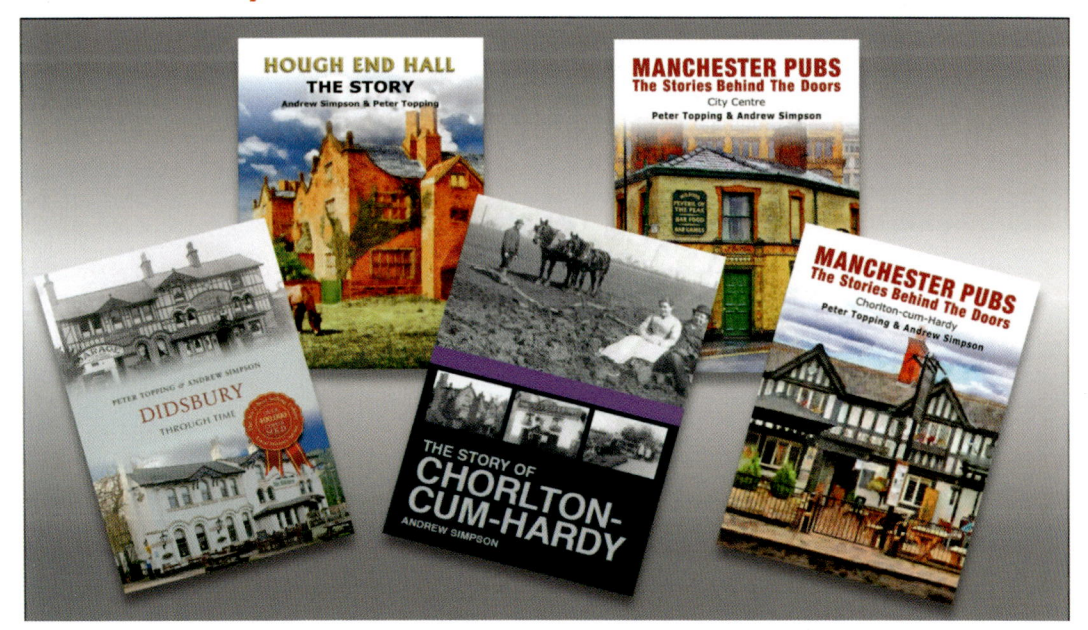

Local artist Peter Topping and historian Andrew Simpson are working together on a series of collaborations including paintings and stories about Chorlton and Manchester. For more information contact us at peter@pubbooks.co.uk or contact Peter on 07521 557888.

195

MANCHESTER PUBS
The Stories Behind The Doors

Chorlton-cum-Hardy

Peter Topping & Andrew Simpson

111 pubs & bars, 21 walks
2 books to choose from

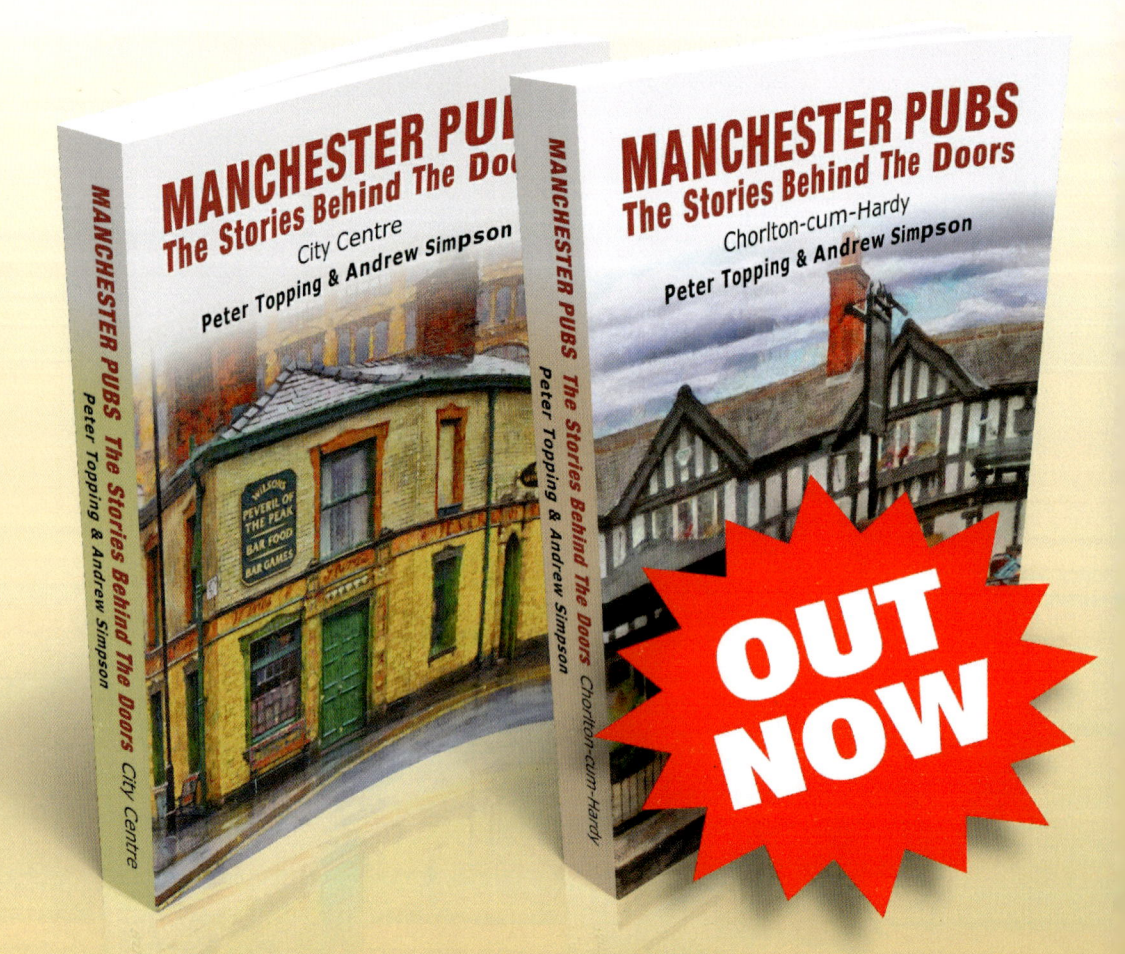

OUT NOW

Web: www.pubbooks.co.uk Email: peter@pubbooks.co.uk
Telephone: 0161 718 0193 Mobile: 07521 557888